Progressive Sight Reading for Classical Guitar
By Dr. Simon Powis

Grades 1 - 8

Dedicated to:

Dr. Alex Guminsky, Dr. Matthew Winter, Dr. George Hruby, Dr. Venu Chalasani, Madeleine Tilley, Nanette Altes, and the incredible oncology nurses, doctors, and staff of Royal North Shore Hospital in Sydney, Australia. Thank you for the care, dedication, and kindness that you provided to me and so many others.

First Edition
Copyright Simon Powis 2023
Published by Classical Guitar Corner Publishing
cgcpublishing.com

The guitar featured on the cover is made by Garrett Lee.
Please support the classical guitar community by purchasing original versions of music.
www.classicalguitarcorner.com

Accompanying materials to this method can be found at
classicalguitarcorner.com/sight-reading

Contents

About Simon Powis

Growing up in Sydney, Australia, Simon undertook his first committed studies to the classical guitar with Raffaele Agostino at the Sydney Conservatorium of Music. Following on from Sydney, Powis studied in various festivals in Europe, the Royal Academy of Music in London, and eventually ended up working with Benjamin Verdery towards a Doctorate in Music at Yale University.

As a performer, Powis has performed internationally in Asia, Australia, the Americas, and Europe. Solo performance highlights include the Kennedy Center, the Adelaide International Guitar Festival, and a solo tour in Beijing. Ensemble collaborations with string quartet, cello, violin, voice, and guitar duos have seen a range of performances and recording with highlights including the GFA Symposium with Ben Verdery, Carnegie Hall with the Linden Quartet, and the Rockport Music Hall with cellist Jacques Lee Wood.

In the past ten years, Powis has increasingly focused on creating a unique approach to online classical guitar education. Classical Guitar Corner and its accompanying Academy provides a variety of educational resources for the public and a comprehensive graded curriculum for students of the Academy. Replete with a podcast, masterclasses, Summer School, articles, tutorial videos, exams, and live performance seminars, Powis serves a large community of classical guitarists around the world. In addition to the online resources Powis has compiled and authored over 12 books including practice routines, graded repertoire, study guides, and sight reading challenges.

Other Publications by Simon Powis

The Cornerstone Method for Classical Guitar
Graded Repertoire for Classical Guitar
20 Practice Routines for Classical Guitar
Graded Duets for Classical Guitar
Complete Major and Minor Scales and Arpeggios
The Classical Guitar Handbook

cgcpublishing.com

About the CGC Academy

The Academy at Classical Guitar Corner has become much more than an online resource to learn classical guitar. It has become a community, a sanctuary for learning, a source of inspiration, and a family.

With a structured approach to learning, students at the Academy benefit from a clear path to progress. That path guides them through the maze of materials that make up the learning process and leaves them feeling positive about music. The feeling of achievement, of success, and of mutual respect fuels further dedicated practice and a virtuous cycle ensues.

If you find that these materials suit your learning style and help you focus in your practice sessions, then I highly encourage you to join the CGC Academy as it is a world class institution filled with people who are passionate about the classical guitar. Learn more at www.classicalguitarcorner.com

Preface

Sight-reading has been a favorite topic of mine over the last fifteen years, starting as the focus of my doctoral thesis and continuing as lectures and further research. My goal has always been to create something that contributes to the existing pedagogy, something practical and effective.

In the fall of 2008 I sat down with Ben Verdery on the lawn in front of the Yale University library. We discussed what might be a good topic for my doctoral thesis, and in the following weeks we decided that sight-reading would be the central theme of my research. The resulting thesis title was: 'Towards a Method for Sight-Reading on Classical Guitar.'

The next two years of research marked the beginning of my interest in pedagogy and ignited a newfound passion for teaching. Sight-reading, a comprehensive skill that integrates various musical elements such as musicianship, theory, and performance skills, led me to explore a wide range of pedagogical subjects. It inspired me to become a more effective teacher. The eventual outcome of all these efforts was the establishment of Classical Guitar Corner Academy, which has now expanded to offer a comprehensive curriculum covering all aspects of classical guitar.

As you might guess, this book holds a special significance for me. It represents a large portion of my professional journey and completes the circle of my research. While my initial research was primarily academic, with this book, I hope to provide a practical and enjoyable resource that assists you in incorporating sight-reading into your regular practice.

Have fun!

Simon Powis

Acknowledgments

This book has undergone a long journey, commencing in 2008 with my doctoral research at Yale and culminating in 2022 with a residency at the Banff Center for the Arts. I extend my gratitude to all the musicians who generously shared their insights, experiences, and wisdom: John Williams, Ben Verdery, Raffaele Agostino, Dr. Janet Agostino, Jerry Willard, David Leisner, Dr. Jennie Shaw, Dave Belcher, and Nicoletta Todesco.

Furthermore, I'd like to express my appreciation to the Banff Center for the Arts and the Leo Brouwer Endowment for facilitating the book-writing process through an artist residency. I also want to thank my wife, Evita, for her unwavering support of my creative endeavors and for sharing my passion for teaching. Lastly, a heartfelt thank you goes out to the numerous students at the Classical Guitar Corner Academy; your presence has been instrumental in my ongoing journey of learning as an educator.

An Introduction to Sight-Reading

I often get asked what the secret is to improving sight-reading. Given that it was the topic of my thesis, I can understand why some might wonder if I had stumbled upon a magic key. Indeed, during the six months of workshops I conducted to test ideas with Yale students, I did try and uncover individual elements that would unlock this elusive skill. However, when it comes down to it, sight-reading is a skill that requires gradual development through time and effort. While we could endlessly discuss the challenges and devise novel solutions, in the end, we need to work with material suited to our skill level and maintain consistent practice.

The value of this book is found in a carefully curated set of progressive materials that build your sight-reading skills while avoiding frustration. You will be guided through numerous frequently-used fingerboard positions and play in common key centers. To maintain practicality, I've omitted some less common positions, keys, and musical elements. If I were to aim for comprehensiveness and encompass every possible rhythm, harmony, and pattern across all positions, you might find yourself holding a much weightier book!

The Challenge of Sight-Reading on Guitar

Is sight-reading on the guitar more challenging compared to other instruments? Yes.

You will find some examples that offer a counter to this simplistic answer, such as music for organ or other equally intricate keyboard music. However, the nature of the guitar fingerboard makes sight-reading particularly challenging. Primarily it is the capacity to play notes in multiple positions combined with chordal and polyphonic textures that affect the difficulty of sight-reading on guitar. Even so, we can still develop our skills to a useful and impactful level.

> *To be objective about it, I would say the guitar is more difficult than other instruments because there are more alternatives. So I think one has to face that, it's not an excuse, it's a fact. With piano, of course, there is only one place that each note can be played. ... I think, on the guitar, first of all, even for individual notes you've got alternatives on different strings and you compound that by a factor of two to three to four, any time you've got to combine that with other notes. If you have a B and an E on open strings, how many different ways could you play those notes together? ... It is more difficult than other instruments, but unfortunately it doesn't mean you shouldn't do it, it is even more reason to do more of it!*
> - John Williams [1]

More than the instrument, though, it is the tendency of classical guitarists to work in isolation that affects our reading skills. One of the best things you can do to improve your sight-reading is to play with other musicians on a regular basis. You will be held accountable for your rhythm and ability to stay with the pulse. Moreover, you will most likely be given new music more frequently than if you were alone playing solo repertoire that tends to get memorized.

This book addresses the difficulty of sight-reading by offering material that starts with simple, achievable passages and progresses incrementally towards challenging passages that span the fingerboard. I recommend that all musicians start at the beginning of the book regardless of level as there are sight-reading skills to be developed apart from the reading challenges.

Sight-reading vs. Reading Music Notation

There is an important but challenging distinction to be made between sight-reading and reading music notation. It is important because it clarifies what this book is for and how it is designed. It is challenging because there are a lot of shared traits between the two skill sets.

I have found that sight-reading as a term is often conflated with the ability to read music notation. It may be that some people come across this book expecting to be taught how to read music from the ground up, starting with what notes appear on each string and how to read the musical staff. For that task I have written The Cornerstone Method for Classical Guitar: Grade 1, which teaches all of the notation skills needed to embark on this course of sight-reading.

This book, however, focuses on sight-reading as a skill that develops the ability to make music upon first reading of a score. This ability prioritizes rhythm over pitch, and 'mistakes' need to be let go as should optimal fingerings so that you can protect the pulse. This shift in priority will allow you to sight-read in an ensemble and stay with the group, it will allow you to get a good overview of how a new piece of music sounds, it will allow you to unlock your knowledge of the fingerboard and fingerings, and it will greatly improve your adaptability in lessons.

It is a challenging distinction to make because there is, in fact, a lot of crossover between sight-reading and learning to read notation. When you learn to read notation you will learn the fingerboard, study rhythms, develop reading fluency, and work on fingerings, all of which are shared components with sight-reading. In your normal notation reading, however, you will also be focusing on eliminating mistakes, solving technical problems, delving deep into expression and analysis, and finding optimal fingerings for your musical ideas. These aspects all need a stop-start approach to playing and therefore sacrifice the pulse in order to prioritize musicianship.

The good news is that all of your efforts, regardless of the semantics of the term sight-reading, will move towards reading and playing fluency. While it might be unrealistic to hope that we can play complex and advanced repertoire at sight, we can most definitely rise to a very useful level that empowers us to play in ensembles, facilitates faster learning and communication, and unlocks a wealth of new and unfamiliar repertoire ready to be explored.

The Benefits of Good Sight-Reading

Developing your sight-reading skills will allow you to enter into a larger world of music making. In ensemble settings you will be able to join in and make music with others as well as being able to listen and interact while you play. In lessons you will have more adaptability to explore fingerings and the ability to start playing anywhere in the score will greatly assist in communication between teacher and student. In your own practice sessions you can explore new and unfamiliar music with ease, move away from the need for memorization, and learn repertoire faster.

While we may have heard amazing tales over the years about musicians who could sight-read entire concert works, for most of us we are working to bring our skill to a level that allows us to interact with the musical world more fluently. The key to progress is regular sight-reading and lots of it.

[1] Taken from a phone interview with John Williams, January 29, 2010

How to Use This Book

I recommend all guitarists, regardless of level, start at the beginning of this book. The book is progressive in difficulty but it also introduces skills and concepts in the beginning of the book that are needed throughout.

The book aligns with the rest of the curriculum at Classical Guitar Corner Academy and you will see references to both Grades and Units. These pertain to the organization of our curriculum into eight Grades and twenty Units. The book can be used in isolation and you do not need to be a member of the Academy to make the materials work. If, however, you are new to reading notation and want to learn how to read music from the very beginning, I recommend completing *The Cornerstone Method for Classical Guitar: Grade 1* before using this book.

This book has four components: concepts, rhythms, progressive lessons, and fingerboard challenges.

Concepts

What you will find in these early lessons are the core concepts that impact your sight-reading experience. They separate sight-reading from normal notation reading and you might want to revisit them on a regular basis to keep each concept top of mind as you progress through the book.

Rhythms

Each Grade has a set of rhythms that are provided for your study. These rhythms are not intended for sight-reading but rather for you to work on before undertaking the progressive lessons in each Grade. The rhythms will prepare you for what is to come in the following lessons.

Progressive Lessons

The progressive lessons offer a substantial amount of material that is organized by key, position, and difficulty. In my own lessons with students I like to start out with either duets or sight-reading and these sight-reading lessons make it easy to dive right into reading as the materials are all laid out for you. The two-page lesson could be used in its entirety or you could just use one exercise. It will differ for each player depending on their playing and reading ability.

For individual practice sessions you can progress through the materials at your own pace and re-visit past materials as you like. The key to improvement is reading material that challenges you on a regular basis.

Fingerboard Challenges

Finding all of the wonderful melodies in this book proved quite a challenge! They had to be just right for the position and difficulty level of each lesson. The good news is that we can squeeze some extra juice out of each melody by transposing them into a new key and playing in various positions.

You will see that each fingerboard challenge has a series of positions listed. These are the positions where you can play each melody. When a position needs an extension or a brief shift out of position you will see "(ext.)" written to indicate "extension".

How the Lessons are Organized

There are sixty-two progressive lessons, all following a similar format. Lessons will often specify a particular position for you to maintain throughout the lesson. You will get the most benefit out of this book if you stay in each position as requested rather than using open strings or shifting positions. In later lessons, position changes and open strings are suggested in the instructions or indicated in the fingering.

Most lessons commence with a key center and a provided scale. This scale encompasses the majority of notes featured in the lesson, along with their corresponding fingerings. I recommend reviewing the scale before you begin sight-reading the individual passages. If a scale is absent, it signifies that the lesson involves multiple key centers.

Following the scale you will find a pitch challenge that is devoid of any rhythmic complexities. These are written to sound tonal so that you can hear when a pitch might be incorrect. However, they are intentionally designed to be unmemorable, so that you can revisit them multiple times.

Musicality is addressed after the pitch exercises, encompassing challenges related to dynamics, articulation, phrasing, and other expressive markings. These passages aim to shift your focus beyond pitch and rhythm, fostering the integration of musicality into the sight-reading process.

Every lesson has at least one melody to play, many of which will likely be familiar to you. These melodies help you to self-correct rhythms and pitch due to their familiarity, and they are a lot of fun to play.

Finally, you will find harmonic passages that start to resemble standard repertoire for the classical guitar. These will likely be the most challenging component of each lesson but they bring together what you have learned in a practical context.

Towards the book's conclusion, lessons feature substantial excerpts or even full pieces of repertoire. This represents the book's final stages, allowing you to put your reading skills to the ultimate test.

Extra Materials

The CGC Academy will host a comprehensive video version of each lesson, accessible to members. If you're not a member, I maintain a dedicated mailing list for sight-reading materials, where I share useful scores and materials I come across.

You can join that mailing list at: **www.classicalguitarcorner.com/sight-reading**

 Terminology
Various terms used in this book

Adagio	Slow
A tempo	Resume previous tempo.
Anacrusis	One or more unstressed notes before the first bar line of a piece or passage.
A piacere	The performer may use their own discretion with regard to tempo and rhythm.
Barcorolle	A Venetian gondolier's song typified by gently rocking rhythms in 6/8 or 12/8 time.
D.C. al Fine	Dal Capo al Fine - Return to the beginning and continue until it is marked "Fine".
D.S. al Fine	Dal Segno al Fine - Return to the segno symbol and continue until "Fine".
Dolce	Sweetly
Extension (ext.)	Indicating that there will be some notes played out of position.
Fermata	A pause of unspecified length on a note or rest.
Flesh tone	Played with the flesh of the finger rather than the nail.
Forte *f*	Loud
Fortissimo *ff*	Very loud.
Largo	Slow and broad.
Ledger Lines	A short line added for notes above or below the range of a stave.
Legato	Smooth and flowing in manner, without breaks between notes.
Maestoso	Majestically, stately.
Mezzo Piano *mp*	Moderately soft.
Mezzo Forte *mf*	Moderately loud.
Moderato	At a moderate speed.
Molto	Very
Mordent	A rapid alternation of a note with the note immediately below or above it.
Morendo	Dying away.
Normale	Normal tone played near the back of the sound hole on the guitar.
Ostinato	A continually repeated musical phrase or rhythm.
Piano *p*	Soft
Pianissimo *pp*	Very soft
Pizzicato (*pizz.*)	Plucking a string while muting the same string with the palm of the hand.
Poco	A little
Ponticello (*pont.*)	Played near the bridge of the guitar
Position	A position refers to a relationship between fingers and frets on the guitar. Fifth position, for example, would indicate the first finger plays the fifth fret, the second finger the sixth, the third finger the seventh, and the fourth finger the eighth.
Ritmico	Rhythmic, rhythmically.
Rallentando (*rall.*)	Gradually decreasing in speed.
Ritenuto (*rit.*)	Held back - indicating an abrupt slowing down.
Subito (*sub.*)	Suddenly
Staccato	A note of shortened duration, separated from the note that may follow by silence.
Step-wise movement	Melodic motion in which the interval between notes is no more than a step.
Tasto	Played near or over the fingerboard of the guitar
Trill	An ornament consisting of a rapid alternation between two adjacent notes.
Transposed	Referring to a collection of pitches moved up or down in pitch by an interval.
Vibrato	A rapid, slight variation in pitch producing a stronger or richer tone.
Voices	Individual musical lines that can be found within a musical texture.

CONCEPTS

Skills for Sight-Reading

In the first three units we will explore six core concepts of sight-reading. Scanning the score, protecting the pulse, looking ahead, dropping out, pattern recognition, and making music.

Each lesson will describe a concept and provide some examples to reinforce the idea. The examples are not intended to be sight-read at this stage but rather help to demonstrate what each concept might look like in a practical setting.

As you move on to Grade Two (Unit 4) you will encounter sight-reading lessons that start at a basic level and progressively get more difficult towards the final lesson in Unit 20. Even if the material seems simple to you I would encourage you to start at the beginning of the book so you can practice using the sight-reading concepts presented here in Grade One.

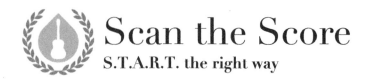

Scan the Score
S.T.A.R.T. the right way

I want you to develop a new habit of scanning the score every time you are about to sight-read because it will greatly improve the quality of your reading.

This scan only needs to take a few seconds and we can remember five simple components with the acronym: **S.T.A.R.T.**

S for Signature

The key **signature** (S) will affect a large number of notes that you are about to read. It will give you a good idea of the key of the piece. Check the key signature at the beginning and quickly scan the beginning of each system to see if it changes at any point.

T for Time

The **time** signature (T) will affect the rhythmic grouping and feel of the piece. Check the time signature and scan the score to see if it changes at any point.

A for About

Take in any information **about** (A) the piece that is presented on the score. This might come in the form of a composer's name, the title, or expression markings at the beginning of the score. If you have more time you can look over the various expression markings in the piece too. A small amount of knowledge can transform your reading because you can access your memory of pieces you know, and styles you are familiar with.

R for Repeats

Repeats (R) can often trip you up when reading if you haven't identified them from the outset. Scan the piece to get a sense of the form, and map out any repeated sections. If you are reading together in an ensemble, it might even be worth marking the repeats on the score so that they are obvious.

T for Tempo

The final element is perhaps the most important. Choosing a manageable **tempo** (T) for your music is crucial to maintaining a steady pulse. What can often catch people off guard is a sudden leap in difficulty with rhythm or harmony. Scan through the score to identify sections that might be the most challenging and choose a suitable tempo based on that material rather than what you might find in the first measures.

Let's try this scanning process on a passage of music. Use the START scan to the best of your ability and we will walk through the process together on the next page.

Not Perfect, but Very Helpful

Scanning the score before you play will always be helpful to your sight-reading. The **START** scan covers the basics of what to look for on your scan but remember that it is not comprehensive and not all pieces will feature every element.

On the following page I have chosen Schubert's *Unfinished Symphony* theme because we could use each element of the **START** scan as an example. However, you will find many pieces will not have certain elements like a repeat, title, or tempo. Other pieces will have much more information to scan such as dynamics, articulations, phrase marks, or tempo changes. Whatever the case, the **START** scan will cover the essentials and by using it every time you sight-read you will be developing a powerful habit that will improve your sight-reading.

Unit 1.1
Classical Guitar Corner Academy

Let's practice using the START scan on a famous melody by Franz Schubert. Go through the scan in order and see what aspects might help you with sight-reading. Compare your notes with the ones I have provided below.

Theme from the Unfinished Symphony - Franz Schubert
Allegro Moderato

Signature

The key signature has one sharp, which would normally indicate either G major or E minor as the key. As the melody begins and ends on the note G, we can assume the melody is in G major.

Time

The time signature is 3/4 and there is no anacrusis.

About

The piece is marked *Allegro Moderato* which helps us plan our tempo. More importantly we can see that this is the famous theme to Schubert's *Unfinished Symphony*. If you are already familiar with the symphony then this information about the melody and its composer will greatly assist in sight-reading.

Repeats

As this is a short melody there is not much to take in about an over-arching form. However, by scanning the score we can see that there is a repeat sign at the end of the melody. Noticing this in the scan will help prepare for a smooth transition back to the first measure.

Tempo

The opening measure has a fairly simple rhythm, which could be sight-read at a moderate to fast tempo. However, as we continue the scan we can see that the rhythm gets more active in the second line and also features dotted eighths with sixteenth notes. A slower starting tempo that accommodates this rhythmic difficulty will help us protect the pulse when we arrive at this passage.

Protect the Pulse

Let it go, let it go...

The priority in sight-reading is to maintain a steady pulse. This means that even if you play the wrong pitch, misread a rhythm, or use a poor fingering you must let it go and forge ahead without losing the pulse.

Mistakes

Your current habit might be to react to a mistake by stopping, going back, and attempting the passage again. However, when sight-reading this will put you out of sync with anyone you might be playing with, it will disturb the flow of the music, and it can sometimes derail the reading process entirely.

The ability to let mistakes go and to protect the pulse is something you will develop over the course of your sight-reading studies. It can actually feel quite liberating to let mistakes go knowing that if you play just the first and last note in time you have been more successful than playing all the correct pitches out of time.

Given that the pulse is the priority, choosing a manageable tempo will be crucial to your success. A common mis-step can be to start sight-reading without scanning the score to see what is coming up. If there is a particularly fast or challenging passage buried several lines down you will need to choose a tempo that suits that passage even if it seems slow for everything else.

Fingering

Fingering on the classical guitar can change the way the music sounds, affect technical challenges, and even contribute to your unique sound as a musician. For these reasons, we can devote a great deal of time and effort to working on musical and efficient fingerings. When it comes to sight-reading, however, you must throw your tendency towards perfection out the window and use whatever works!

Sight-reading doesn't afford us the time to figure out the best fingerings and so we will often need to use whatever fingers are available to keep the music going. Hopping around on one finger, excessive shifting and dropping out notes will be some of the ways you navigate fingering choices while sight-reading.

The better you know the fingerboard the more fluent and logical your fingering will be. This book will help you develop your fingerboard knowledge by providing you with customized passages that keep you in position. Most guitarists will drop down to first position as soon as possible in order to avoid difficulty, but this means that the upper positions remain under developed. As you go through the lessons in this book make sure you play in the indicated positions because it will strengthen your knowledge of the fingerboard and therefore help your fingering choices.

One of the sight-reading difficulties that sets the guitar apart from some other instruments is the need to shift into different positions in order to play a passage. A common scenario might see you playing in first position and then suddenly a high note appears on the first string and it seems like you should have been playing in a higher position all along. The result of this is usually a hesitation and therefore disruption of the pulse. The only way to counter this, besides scanning the score at the outset, is to develop your ability to look ahead in the music. Looking ahead will give you time to make shifting and fingering choices that allow the pulse to be protected.

As you develop your skills, your right- and left-hand fingering habits will help you be more fluent and elegant with on-the-fly fingering. But don't be too hard on yourself if it feels clunky in the early stages of sight-reading, just let it go and go protect the pulse at all costs.

Unit 1.2
Classical Guitar Corner Academy

In the following three exercises you will find some notes are missing. In fact, in exercise three, you will find an entire measure is missing. What I would like you to do is fill in the missing notes by playing whatever you like. As long as you come in on the next written note in time you will have been successful. What we are practicing here is the ability to play a wrong note, let it go, and move on to the next note. If you want to have some extra fun, make the wrong notes as wrong as possible!

In exercise four and five I want you to choose a tempo that makes sight-reading easy. Choose a tempo so slow that it is impossible to make a mistake.

When choosing your tempo take into consideration the eighth notes in measure three.

Remember that you control the speed of the sixteenth notes with your tempo.

Sight-reading doesn't always allow enough time to make the best fingering choices, so you have to do the best you can in the moment. Play through both exercise six and seven knowing that even though the second set of fingerings is better, the first is acceptable when sight-reading at a beginner level.

When in Doubt, Drop Out

It is better not to play than to play out of time

A skill that is quite unique to sight-reading is the ability to skip notes, thin out harmonies, or even drop out all together when playing. There will almost always be a few difficult moments in a piece that can stall your sight-reading and because the goal is to protect the pulse, the ability to drop out and re-enter the flow of music while maintaining the pulse is an important skill to develop.

Skipping notes

Some pitches will be harder to read than others. Ledger lines and certain flat notes are probably the most common examples where one note might prove more difficult than others. In this case it is an option to simply drop that note out and continue playing, in time, with the following note.

Rhythm can pose a similar problem when an uncommon or complex rhythmic figure appears in the music. In this instance you can simplify the rhythm down to the first note that falls on the beat. You will see in the following example that the dotted rhythms have been simplified to half notes, removing some difficulty.

Thinning out harmony

Stacked chords, especially uncommon ones, can cause a hesitation in reading as we not only try and read the pitches but also try and find a fingering to accommodate the chord. To prioritize the pulse you can remove notes from the harmony until it becomes easy enough to play in time. It is up to you which notes you prioritize and each situation will be different. In general it will be best to keep either the lowest or highest note.

Dropping out altogether

Sometimes it is better to simply stop playing altogether. This can be particularly useful in an ensemble setting because if you are lost, or out of time with the rest of the group, you will affect the sound of the entire group. Although you might drop out it is still your job to stay with the music as best you can and aim to re-enter when it is possible. Good places to re-join might be a musical cue like a repeat or a pause or you could look to your colleagues for guidance. Even though it might not feel like it, playing the first and last note together with nothing else in between is more successful than playing the right pitches at the wrong time. The following example displays a thinning out of the harmony and dropping out until the end.

Unit 2.1
Classical Guitar Corner Academy

The first two exercises contain rhythms and notes that might challenge your ability to maintain the pulse when sight-reading. Play through the passages and omit any challenging notes. For the first exercise, you can play the pitch on each beat while excluding the sixteenth notes. In the second exercise, refrain from playing the notes with unfamiliar accidentals; insert a rest instead and continue to the next note in time.

In exercise three, there are two voices that are indicated with note stems going in opposite directions. Choose just one voice to play for this passage. In ensemble playing, when a single part is split between players, this is referred to as 'divisi.' In exercise four, you will find a variety of ways to thin out the texture. Try a few different approaches and decide what would best preserve the music.

In an ensemble it is better to drop out than to play the correct pitch at the wrong time. The challenge is to keep your place in the music without losing the beat and to re-join when you are able. In exercise five we will simulate this process by intentionally dropping out and re-joining as indicated. The familiar melody will help you to keep track of the music.

Look Ahead
Reading ahead of where you are playing

In 2003 I spent one year studying at the Royal Academy of Music in London. To help pay the bills I worked at Wigmore Hall as a page turner. This rather obscure job, which has likely been phased out by iPads and foot pedals, meant that I got a first-hand look at the ability of professional pianists to look ahead as they were reading music.

The interaction between pianist and page turner is quite subtle and it simply involves a tiny nod of the head to signal that the page needs to be turned. Every player was different: some would read a few measures ahead, some would be several lines of music ahead, and some would live life on the edge and nod their head just as the music was about to finish at the bottom of the page.

As a sight-reader you will need to develop the ability to read ahead because by the time the music on the page matches what you are playing it is too late to get your fingers in position. Perhaps more than other instruments, the guitar needs extra time to plan how to arrange the fingers and when to shift because of the compounding effects of string choices and harmony.

Reading ahead of where you are playing can feel very odd when starting out, but as you develop this skill, you will be able to take in chunks of information at a time and skip ahead. The ability to look ahead in the music incorporates aural skills, harmonic knowledge, familiarity with the style, composer, and genre, and the ability to both recognize and predict patterns. It will take time and experience to develop this skill to a high level, but there are some accessible starting points.

Scanning the Score

The first opportunity to look ahead will be in your initial scan of the score. This is an opportunity to identify where and when you can deploy the various sight-reading concepts. Even if you have just ten seconds to scan before playing, you can identify a variety of elements that might normally derail the sight-reading process.

Long Notes

Once you have played a note, you do not need to look at it while it is still sounding. Long notes provide a fantastic way to develop the habit of moving your eyes ahead of where you are playing in the music. With just one piece of information to process, you can focus on maintaining the pulse and moving to the next note. The early lessons in this book offer many opportunities to develop this skill, and I encourage you to increase the challenge of simple exercises by trying to take in several notes, or even measures, as you play through the exercises.

Repeated Notes

Similar to a long note duration, a repeated note does not need your eyes to stay in the same place. There is more information to process because you will need to take in the number of notes and the rhythm. What you are effectively doing is chunking several pieces of information into one. This is the beginning of pattern recognition.

Patterns

Pattern recognition, which we will continue to explore in the following lesson, allows you to take in larger chunks of information at a time. It helps us in a similar way that long or repeated notes do, in that we can move our eyes ahead once we have recognized a pattern. It takes a little more experience to use patterns in sight-reading, but you can start with simple rhythmic patterns or melodic patterns and move to more complex patterns that involve harmony and arpeggios.

Unit 2.2
Classical Guitar Corner Academy

Practice looking ahead by moving your eyes as soon as you have played each note but make sure you hold the note for its full duration. Repeat the exercise and see how far ahead you can read while playing in time.

1

2

Move your eyes ahead as soon as you have played the first note of each repeated group.

3

4

Rhythmic, melodic, and harmonic patterns can be grouped or "chunked" into one idea. See if you can chunk some of these rhythms and pitch patterns and move your eyes ahead as soon as possible.

5

6

Pattern Recognition
Chunking your music can help you read

Patterns are everywhere in music. You will find patterns in melody with repeated pitches and melodic fragments, in rhythm and articulation with repetition, and in harmony with arpeggiation. Some patterns are obvious, like a repeated rhythm, and some are a bit more elusive, like an arpeggiated chord, but once identified they will all help with your reading fluency.

Good sight-readers will be able to chunk information in the music and make the most of any patterns that occur. Chunking occurs naturally. For instance, the words you are reading right now are being chunked. Only when you come up against a brand new word (perhaps a neologism) do you actually sound out all the letters to form the word in your mind. This tendency to rely on patterns is so strong that the brain sometimes fills in gaps automatically. A fun eaxpmle of tihs cna be fonud in a sntecne taht has letrtes in the miledde of ecah wrod mxeid up.

Below you will find some examples of musical material that can be chunked together to help sight-reading.

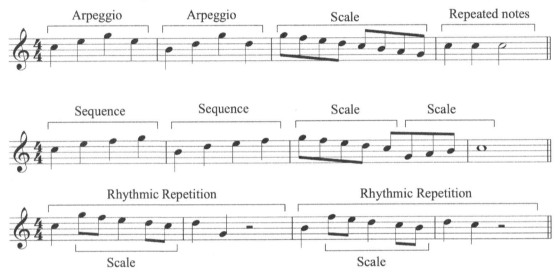

Not all music will fit so neatly into different chunks like the examples above, so let's take an excerpt from Coste's *Lesson 24* to see what patterns might help us in the sight-reading process.

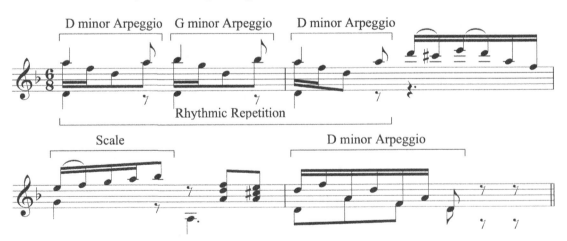

Sight-reading is a comprehensive skill that is impacted by your overall knowledge and experience as a musician. As you learn more about harmony, stylistic features of a period, and develop an in-depth knowledge of specific composers, your sight-reading will increasingly benefit from pattern recognition and chunking. In fact, at an advanced level, sight-reading will use pattern prediction as part of the process. With so many common harmonic and melodic progressions in western classical music, prediction can blend with improvisation to create a seemingly magical ability to realize music at first sight.

Unit 3.1
Classical Guitar Corner Academy

Almost all music that you come across will have patterns that can help your sight-reading. Go through each of the five examples below and see what kind of patterns might help you in the sight-reading process. Look for scale fragments, harmonic progressions, arpeggiated chords, repetitive rhythms, and repetitive articulations.

Barcarolle Op.51 No. 1 - Napoléon Coste

Always Make Music
Sight-reading is more than pitch + rhythm

Pitch and rhythm are challenging enough to sight-read let alone having to add musicality and expression but that is what we will aspire to do as sight-readers.

Incorporating Expressive Markings

When you read a musical score there are often many more symbols and instructions on the page apart from the notes. Dynamics, articulations, tempo changes, expression markings, and phrases can all be used to inform how to interpret the music. We need to incorporate as much expression as possible into sight-reading otherwise we are missing out on making music.

The first step is to scan the score and look for any expression or articulation markings. As you scan, see if you can get a sense for the shape of each musical phrase and the overall musical idea.

As you develop your reading and aural skills you will be able to "hear" what the music sounds like in your head and this will prepare you for a successful reading of the music.

The most important goal is to play with musical expression right from the start. As we have mentioned several times now, don't worry about perfection but rather do the best you can.

Take a look at the example below that has grayed-out notes and notice how many expressive markings are present beyond pitch and rhythm.

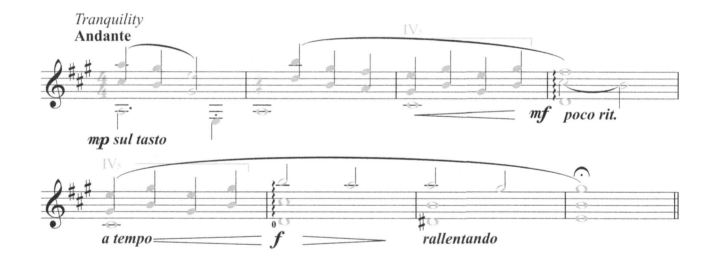

Playing Expressively Without Expressive Markings

On the other end of the spectrum you will encounter music that has little to no expressive markings to guide your interpretation. This does not mean, however, that you should play without expression. Rather, you will need to draw on your stylistic knowledge and musical creativity to shape the music while sight-reading.

Because you will not know the music you are sight-reading it is quite possible that you might make some expressive choices that don't seem to work. This is normal and to be expected. Be creative and take some risks in your expression.

Unit 3.2
Classical Guitar Corner Academy

In the first melody your challenge is to incorporate the composer's expressive markings into your sight-reading. This is more challenging than reading just pitch and rhythm but you should always aim to include as much expression as possible from the outset.

Tempo de Vals noble from *Valses Poeticos* - Enrique Granados

In the second melody you are not provided with any expressive direction. Nevertheless, you must draw upon all of your musical intuition and understanding to play the music with expression. You can use a variety of expressive elements such as dynamics, articulation, tone colors, and tempo.

Since the melody originates from the same composer and piece as the previous passage, you can draw upon your musical knowledge and experience to guide your decisions. As you accrue more musical experience you will be able to develop an intuitive approach to interpretation that encompasses a wide variety of styles and periods.

Melodico from *Valses Poeticos* - Enrique Granados

PROGRESSIVE LESSONS

The progressive lessons offer a substantial amount of material organized by key, position, and difficulty. In my own lessons with students, I like to start out with either duets or sight-reading. These sight-reading lessons make it easy to dive right into reading, as the materials are all laid out for you.

The two-page lesson could be used in its entirety, or you could just use one exercise. This will vary for each player based on their playing and reading abilities.

For individual practice sessions, you can progress through the materials at your own pace and revisit past materials as you like. The key to improvement is reading material that challenges you on a regular basis.

Grade 2 Rhythms
Classical Guitar Corner Academy

Clap or play these rhythms on an open string.
You can use a metronome to keep a steady tempo and if you can, count the subdivisions out loud.
Master each rhythm so that you are prepared for the following sight-reading exercises in this unit.

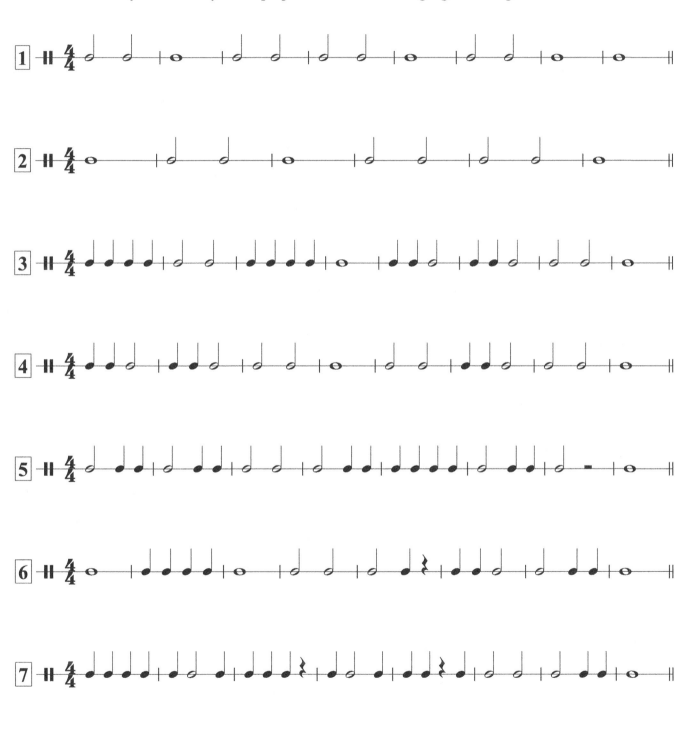

Unit 4.1
Classical Guitar Corner Academy
Play all exercises in 1st position

C Major - 1st Position

Count in at a slow and steady tempo. As soon as you play one note move your eyes to the next.

Although there are half-notes in this passage, the pitch is repeated so you can still move your eyes forward to the next measure after you have played the first note.

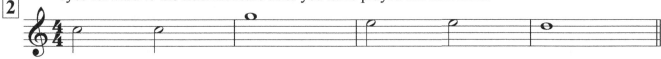

Before you play this passage look at the contour of the notes. They move by step just like a scale. Instead of reading each note separately, think of the four measures as a partial scale.

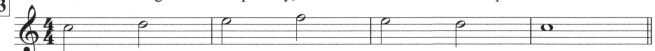

Can you recognize a pattern of intervals between each pair of notes in a measure?

Ledger lines can be tricky to read, choose a slow tempo that will allow you to maintain the pulse.

Follow the fingering provided to avoid hopping with one finger across strings.

6

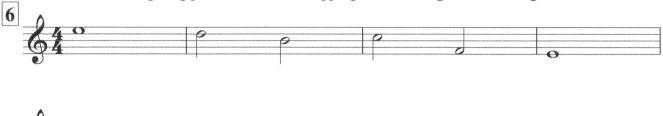

Incorporating dynamics into your sight-reading adds a layer of complexity but it also allows you to make your sight-reading more musical and expressive. Read over the music before starting and take a slow tempo that gives you ample time to control the dynamics in this passage.

7

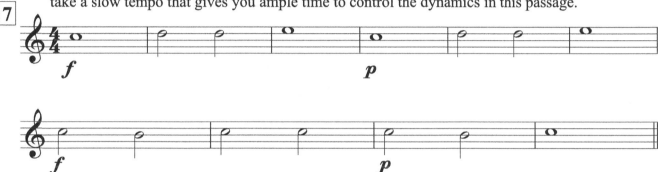

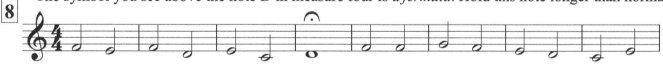

Dies Irae - Gregorian Chant
The symbol you see above the note D in measure four is a *fermata*. Hold this note longer than normal.

8

Play these passages in free time, taking as long as you need to play each pair of notes.
As soon as you play move your eyes to the next measure.

9

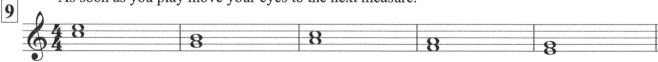

10

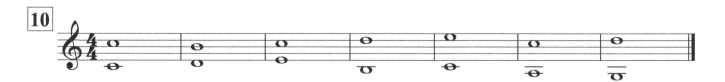

Unit 4.2
Classical Guitar Corner Academy
Play all exercises in 1st position

G Major - 1st Position

Don't forget to look at the key signature!

Scan this passage for accidentals before you start.

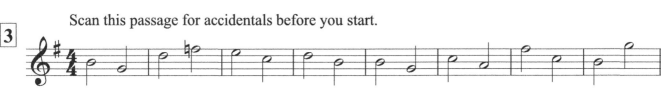

Ledger lines can be challenging to sight-read. Take a slow tempo to protect the pulse.

Phrase marks can help make sense of a musical passage.
Shape the melody using dynamics and subtle *tempo rubato* based on the phrases.

Canon in D - Johann Pachelbel
Scan this passage to S.T.A.R.T. the right way.

The key to reading harmonic passages fluently is a slow tempo, looking ahead, and dropping out notes when needed.

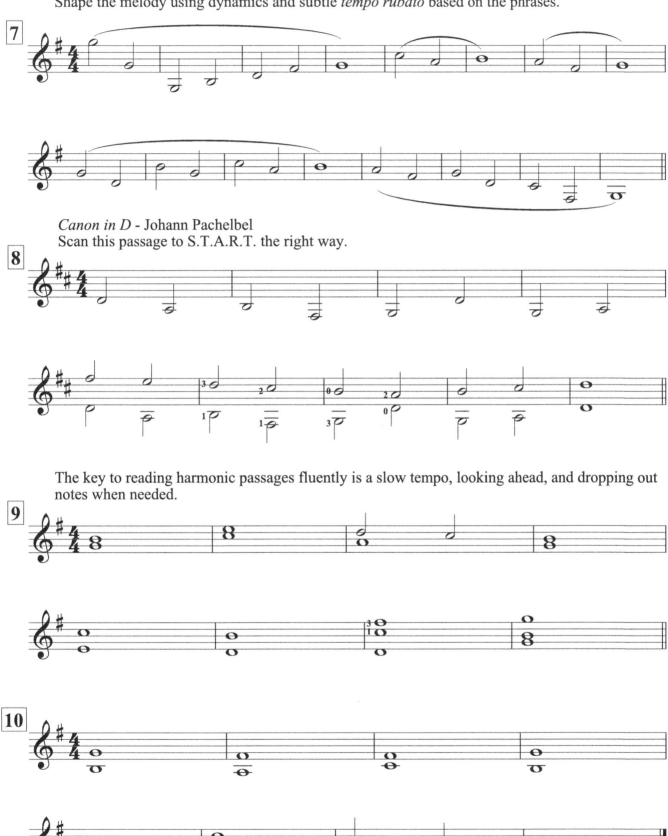

Unit 5.1
Classical Guitar Corner Academy
Play all exercises in 1st position

G Major - 1st Position

1

Can you identify any rhythmic patterns in this passage before you start?

2

You will find both rhythmic and melodic patterns in this passage. Find them before you play and it will help you read with fluency.

3

Take time to clap the rhythm in this passage because it has some syncopation.
Once you have learned the repeated rhythmic pattern you will have an easier time sight-reading.

New World Theme - Antonin Dvořák

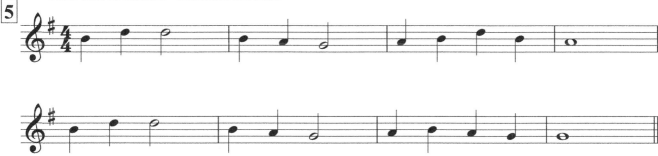

Many of these harmonies use the same left-hand finger from one measure to the next.
Keep fingers down between harmonies when appropriate.

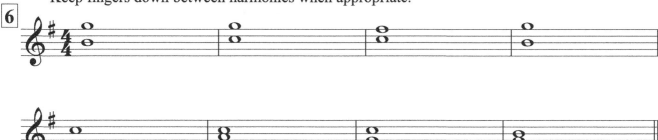

The line between notes in measure 5 indicates that you should shift the second finger from F# to G.
This fingering will briefly take you into second position.

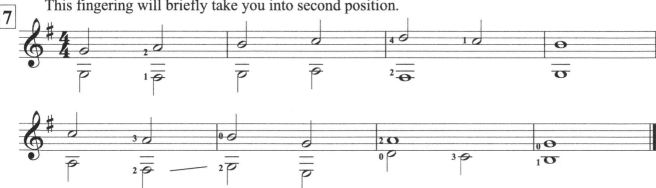

Unit 5.2
Classical Guitar Corner Academy
Play all exercises in 1st position

F Major - 1st Position

Take a moment to find all the Bb's that are in this passage.

1

Choose a tempo that will give you enough time to read the ledger lines in time.

2

Rests are just as important as played notes.
Make sure to play a silence when a rest is indicated by stopping the string from ringing.

3

This melody appeared in the previous lesson. Here, it has been transposed down a whole step to the key of F Major. While the rhythm and melodic shape are identical, the fingering challenges in this key are different. Use your fourth finger to play notes on the third fret, which will prevent hopping around from string to string on the same finger.

4

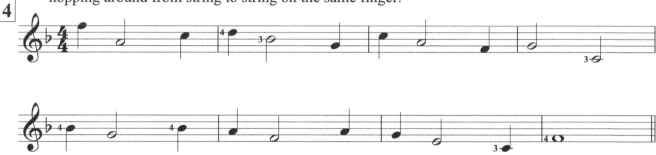

Phrase marks indicate a musical idea by grouping together a series of notes. These notes should be played in a way that reflects their connection and expresses a complete musical thought. A phrase mark can connect just two notes or more.

5

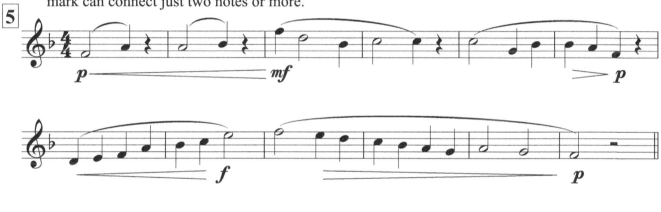

Surprise Symphony - Joseph Haydn

6

As often happens in music, the faster rhythms occur towards the end of the passage. Choose a tempo based on the faster rhythms so that you can maintain a steady pulse.

7

Grade 3 Rhythms
Classical Guitar Corner Academy

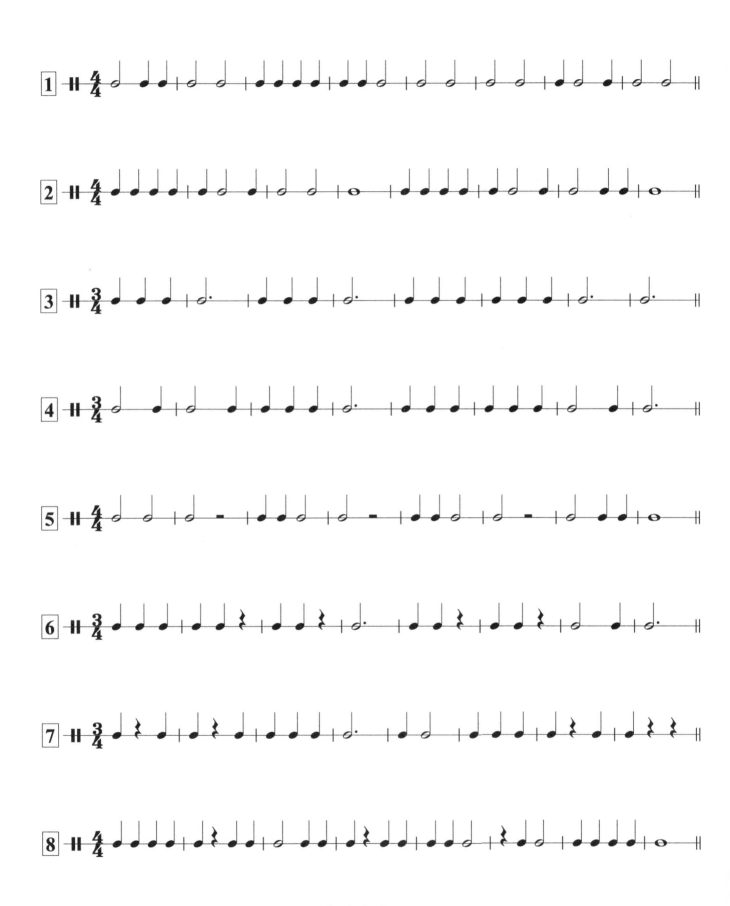

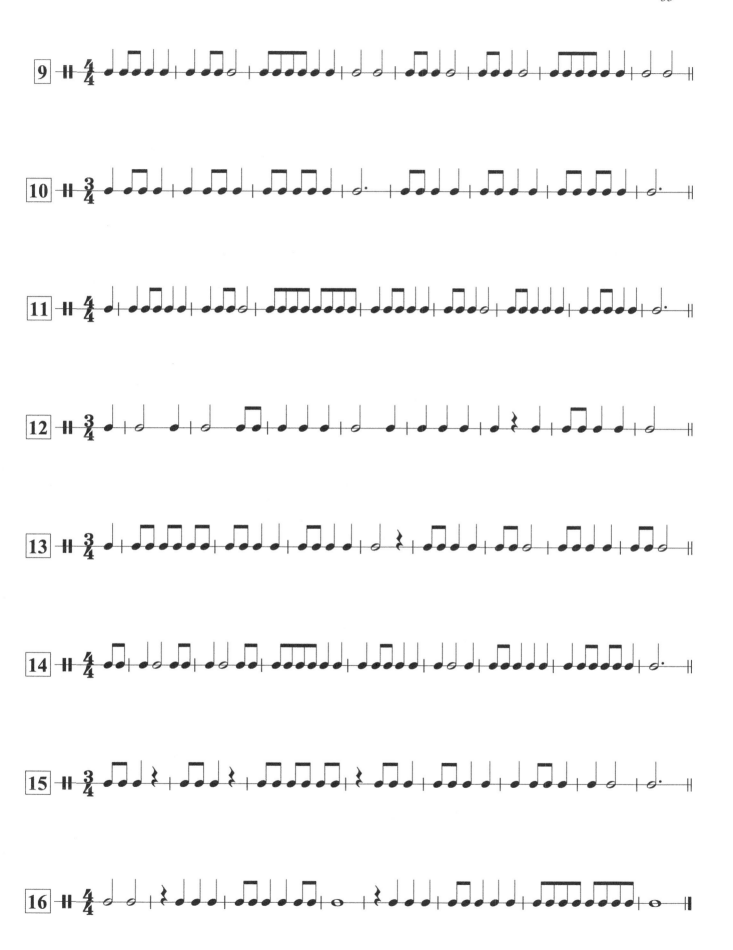

Unit 6.1
Classical Guitar Corner Academy
Play all exercises in 1st position

A Harmonic Minor - 1st Position

Remember that accidentals affect all notes of the same pitch in a single measure.

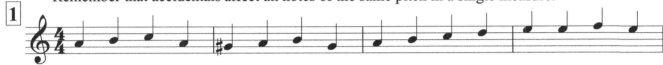

This passage uses the Melodic Minor scale, which raises the 6th and 7th degree (F and G) when ascending and lowers them when descending.

Make sure to check the time signature!

Trick or Treat
Use soft dynamics and a warm tone to create a spooky feel.
Scan the score and START the right way.

6

Unfinished Symphony - Franz Schubert

7

Malagueña - Traditional Spanish

8

"Chunking" chords is a form of pattern recognition. Look at each measure and see if you can recognize any chord shapes or harmonies. If you can chunk a measure at a time, look ahead.

9

Unit 6.2
Classical Guitar Corner Academy
Play all exercises in 1st position

D Harmonic Minor- 1st Position

Scan the passage and note the accidentals before you start.

Shape the following melody with the phasing provided.

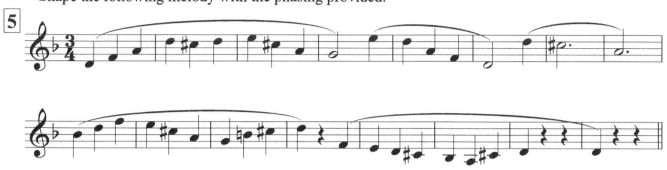

Song of the Volga Boatmen - Traditional Russian
Scan the score and START the right way.

Scan the score and notice the descending bass line that repeats in the first three systems.
As you play each block chord, immediately move your eyes and look ahead to the next measure
and when the harmonies are arpeggiated "chunk" each measure whenever possible.
Take into account the quarter notes when choosing your starting tempo.

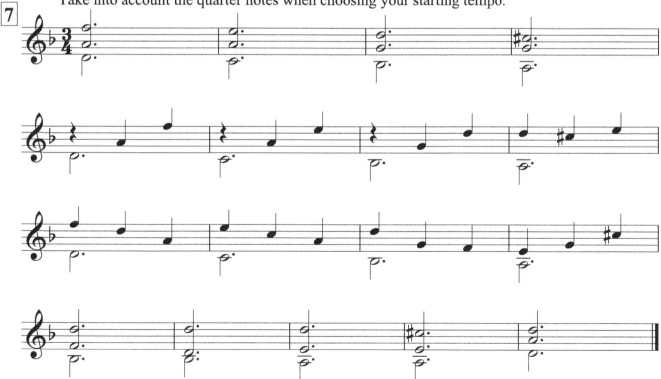

Unit 7.1
Classical Guitar Corner Academy
Play all exercises in 1st position

E Harmonic Minor - 1st Position

The left-hand fingering is quite congested in this passage. When it comes to sight-reading use whatever works in the moment and don't sacrifice the pulse in order to get the best fingering.

Aim to create very clear and deliberate dynamic changes on your first reading.

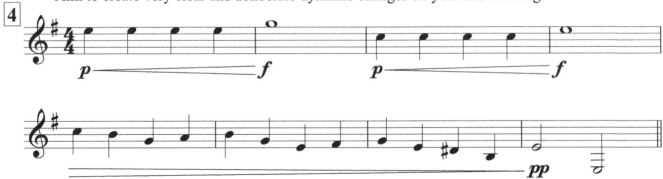

Romanza - Anon.
This passage uses the melody from *Romanza*, however, the accompaniment and bass have been removed and the melody has been transposed down an octave. Shape this beautiful melody with expressive tools such as dynamics, tempo, and tone.

5

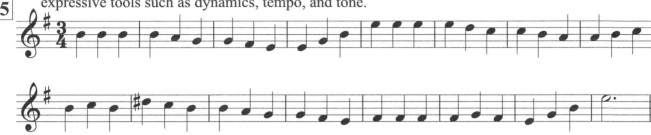

Scan this passage and notice all of the repeated bass notes.

6

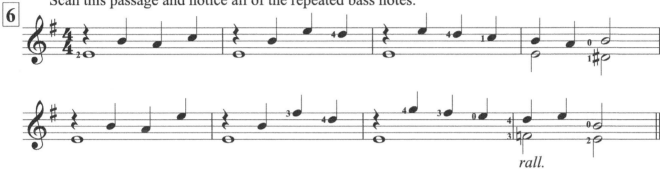

Reading four-note chords might prove too much of a challenge while maintaining a steady pulse. Use the skill of dropping notes out to prioritize the pulse when playing. This could be as extreme as playing just the bass note from each chord. When in doubt, drop out!

7

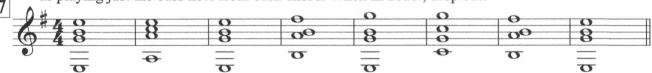

By chunking these notes together you will notice that they are, in fact, the same chords as the previous exercise. In this way you will be reading eight chords instead of thirty-two notes.

8

9

Unit 7.2
Classical Guitar Corner Academy
Play all exercises in 1st position

E Major - 1st Position

The slurs in this passage are used to emphasize the musical "lean" of a non-chordal tone going to a chord tone. Think of this as tension to relaxation and use the slurs to bring out this effect.

Aura Lee - Traditional American
Scan the music and START the right way.

Take a slow tempo and when in doubt, drop out!

These arpeggiated harmonies relate to the passage above.
Chunk these chords to help you sight-read.

Unit 8.1
Classical Guitar Corner Academy
Play all exercises in 1st position

You will find a variety of key signatures and time signatures throughout this lesson.
Scan the score before each passage.

Waltz in A minor
The *staccato* articulations in this piece are typical for a European waltz. If you get stuck with
some of the chords with moving bass lines, simply drop out the chord and play the bass.

Spring from the Four Seasons - Antonio Vivaldi
Scan the score to START the right way.
Use the B on the third string throughout the melody and notice the anacrusis.

What do you consider the most important element in the next passage, chords or the bass line?
If you need to drop out some notes to protect the pulse, prioritize the most important element.

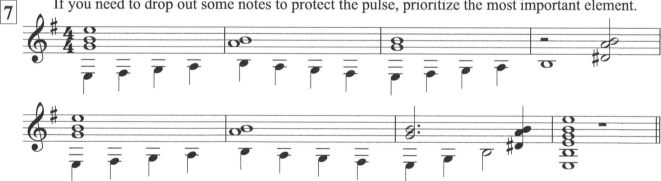

There are multiple sight-reading tactics that will help you with this passage: Take a slow tempo to
prioritize the pulse, chunk the passage to recognize chord patterns, and drop out notes when needed.

Unit 8.2
Classical Guitar Corner Academy
Play all exercises in 1st position

You will find a variety of key signatures and time signatures throughout this lesson.
Scan the score before each passage.

Incorporate the slurs in this passage to give a lilting lead-in to each phrase.

Anitra's Dance - Edvard Grieg
This melody contains *staccato* articulations and a chromatic passage starting in measure nine.
Pretend that you are in an ensemble and you have 30 seconds before you start. Use that time to look
over the music starting at measure nine. When in doubt, drop out!

This passage features a descending chromatic bassline. Bring out the bass and sustain each note
for its full duration by keeping your left-hand finger down.

Aura Lee - Traditional American
This harmonization of Aura Lee is a step up in difficulty because of the moving vocies.
If you need to drop out notes, prioritize the melody in the upper voice.

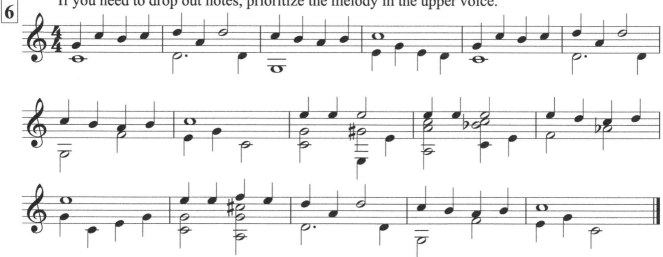

Grade 4 Rhythms
Classical Guitar Corner Academy

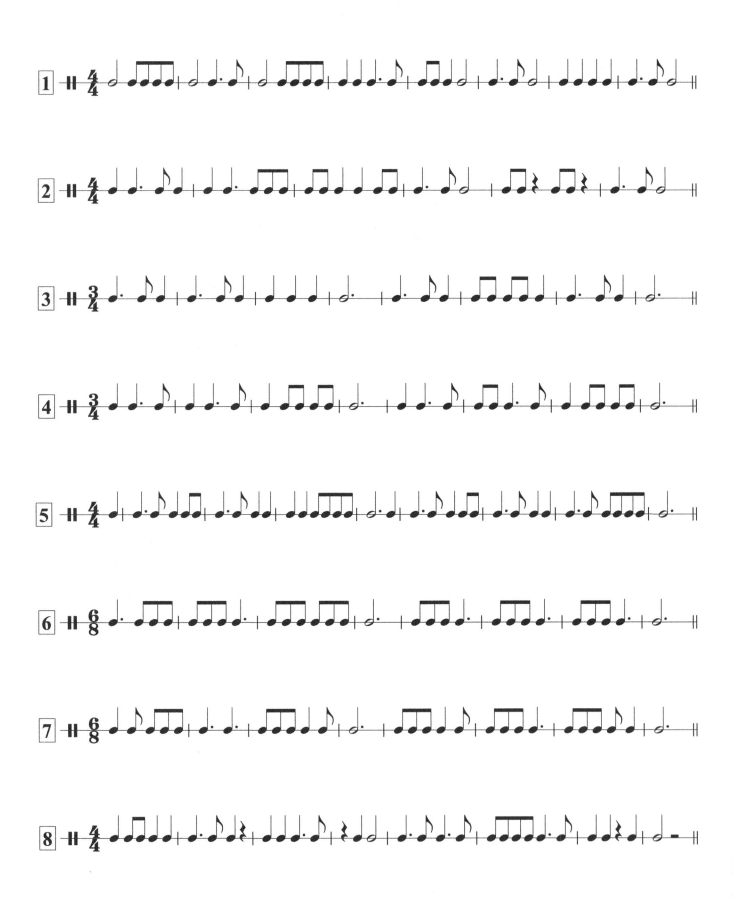

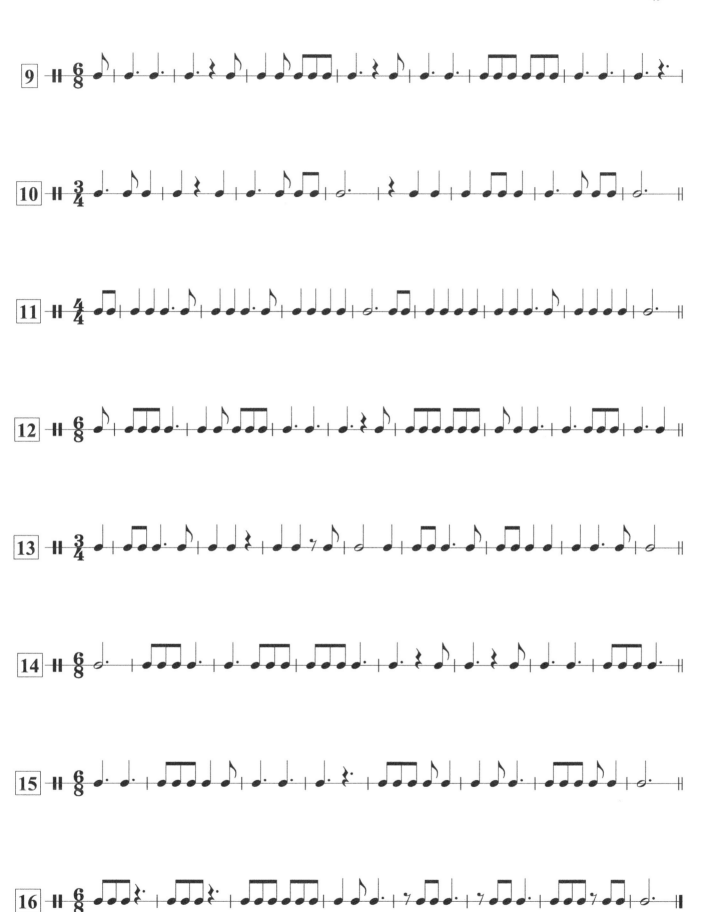

Unit 9.1
Classical Guitar Corner Academy
Play all exercises in 5th position

C Major - 5th Position

You might be wondering why these exercises are suddenly simpler that the previous lessons?
This is because we now moved out of first position.

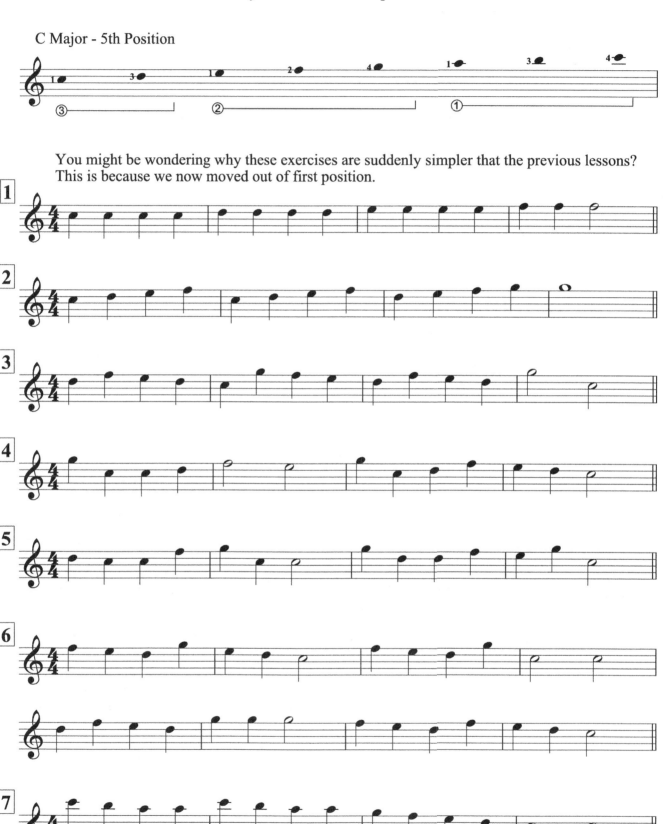

Look over this passage before you start to observe the dynamics.

Twinkle Twinkle Little Star -Traditional

Unit 9.2
Classical Guitar Corner Academy
Play all exercises in 5th position

C Major - 5th Position

This melody has added some eighth-note embellishments to the one above.
Use subdivision to help keep the rhythm steady.

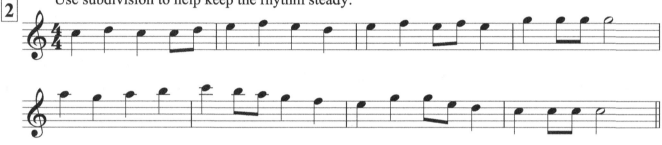

Barres will often be useful in sight-reading to avoid hopping across strings with one finger.
Use a barre over three strings as indicated in this passage.

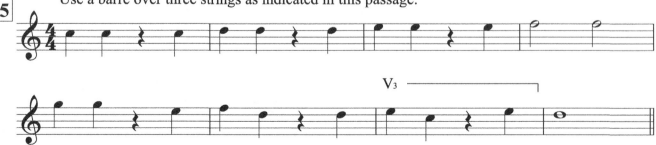

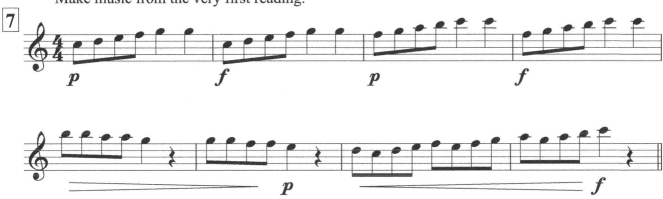

Create as much contrast as you can between the *forte* and *piano* dynamic markings.
Make music from the very first reading.

Kookaburra Sits in the Old Gum Tree -Traditional Australian
There are two good opportunities to use a barre in this melody.
See if you can find them before you start.

Unit 9.3
Classical Guitar Corner Academy
Play all exercises in 5th position

F Major - 5th Position

1

If this dotted rhythm is preventing you from sight-reading fluently, spend some time working on it in the rhythmic exercises for this grade.

2

Chose a tempo based off the eighth-note scale passages.

3

Pastoral
Phrase this passage as indicated by using subtle *rubato* and dynamic swells.

Rujero - Gaspar Sanz
Look for opportunities to be musically expressive, even on the first reading.

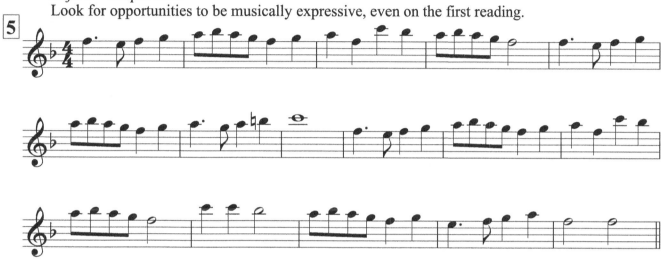

Ode to Joy - Ludwig van Beethoven
Ledger lines can make reading a passage more difficult. In this famous melody use the step-wise movement and your knowledge of the tune to help you sight-read. Before you begin, play through the scale at the beginning of this lesson.

Use barres in the next two passages to help with fingering.

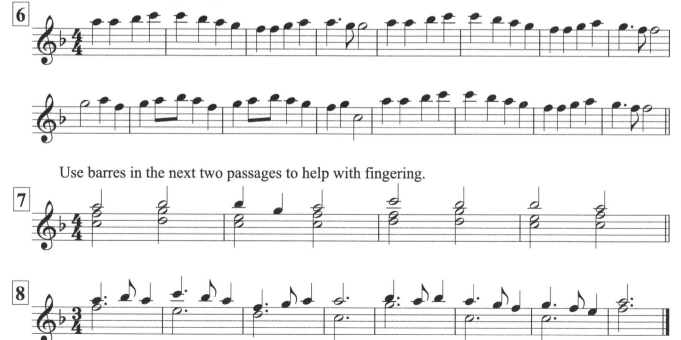

Unit 9.4
Classical Guitar Corner Academy
Play all exercises in 5th position

F Major - 5th Position

Scan through the music before you begin to observe the dynamic markings and accidentals.

Yankee Doodle -Traditional
The next three melodies use simple and well-known folk tunes.
If you want to challenge yourself, take them at a faster tempo.

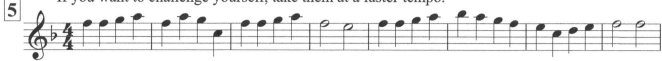

Camptown Races -Stephen Foster

Amazing Grace -Traditional

This passage has some tricky fingering that takes you into sixth position.
Take a slow tempo and when in doubt, drop out!

Unit 10.1
Classical Guitar Corner Academy
Play all exercises in 2nd position

A Major - 2nd Position

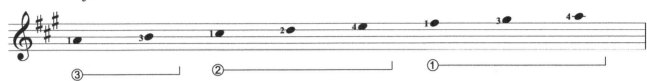

Make sure to stay in second position and refrain from using open strings.

1

Can you find a sequence in this melody before you start? Does it use step-wise movement or leaps?

2

Clap the rhythm of this exercise and count subdivisions out loud before you play.
Take note of the repetitive rhythm and don't forget to read the time signature.

3

Look for repetition to help you. Take note of the dynamics as you play.
Be sure to hold long notes for their full duration.

4

5

Look for all the articulation markings in this exercise.
Can you hear what they sound like in your head before you play?

Spend a few moments working on the fingering and rhythms found in measures five and six before you start to play.

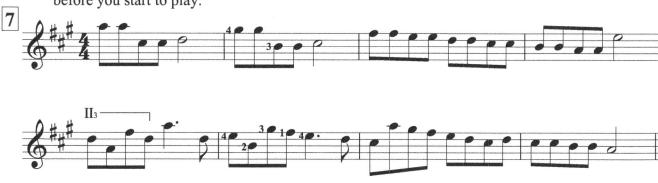

Oh, Susanna - American Folk Song

Take a slow, comfortable tempo and look ahead each time you play a pair of notes.
Feel free to use barres to help with fingering.

This exercise builds on the last and has added movement in the upper and lower voices.

Unit 10.2
Classical Guitar Corner Academy
Play all exercises in 2nd position

D Major - 2nd Position

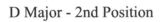

Remember that you control the speed of the eighth notes by your choice of tempo.

1

Take a moment to clap through the rhythms of exercises two, three, five, and eight.

2

3

Scan the score and START the right way.

4

www.classicalguitarcorner.com

Plaisir d'amour- Jean Paul Martini
Counting yourself in with eighth-note subdivisions will help you place the anacrusis correctly.

5

Simple Gifts- Joseph Brackett
Try and hear this melody in your head before you play. Let this mental "audiation" help with your choice of tempo.

6

Play these passages at a slow, calm tempo.
Use the time between notes to look ahead and plan your fingering.

7

Take a slow tempo. When in doubt, drop out.

8

Unit 10.3
Classical Guitar Corner Academy
Play all exercises in 2nd position

B Harmonic Minor - 2nd Position

1

2

El Testament D'Ameila - Traditional Catalan

This haunting melody can be phrased in four or eight measures.
Shape the music with the indicated phrasing as you read.

3

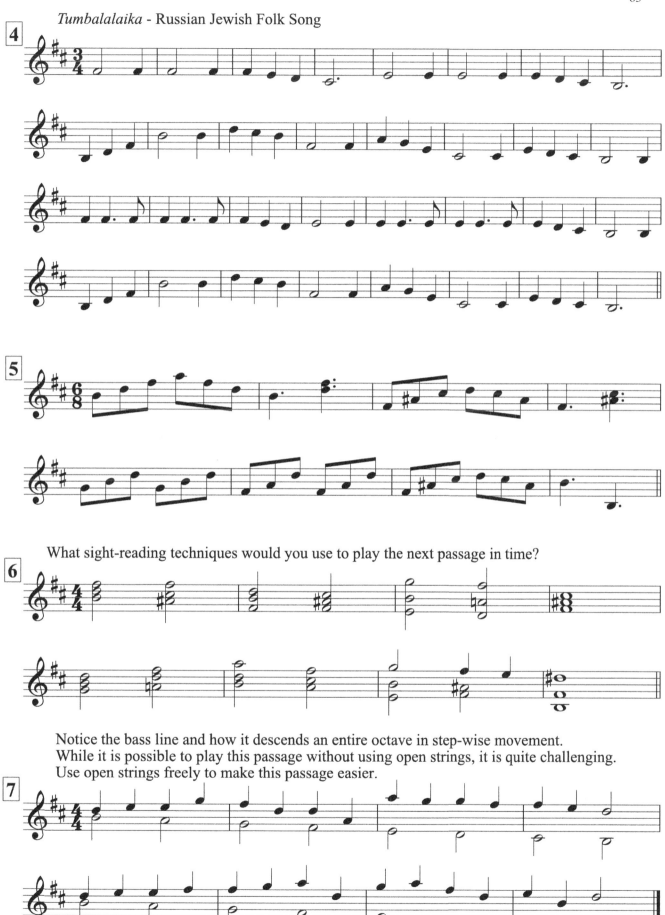

Tumbalalaika - Russian Jewish Folk Song

What sight-reading techniques would you use to play the next passage in time?

Notice the bass line and how it descends an entire octave in step-wise movement.
While it is possible to play this passage without using open strings, it is quite challenging.
Use open strings freely to make this passage easier.

Unit 10.4
Classical Guitar Corner Academy
Play all exercises in 2nd position

Use open strings freely throughout this lesson but remain in the second position.

Barcarolle
Scan the score to START the right way.
Use as many open stings as you can to create resonance and let the music flow.

Bury Me Beneath the Willow Tree - Traditional American

Grade 5 Rhythms
Classical Guitar Corner Academy

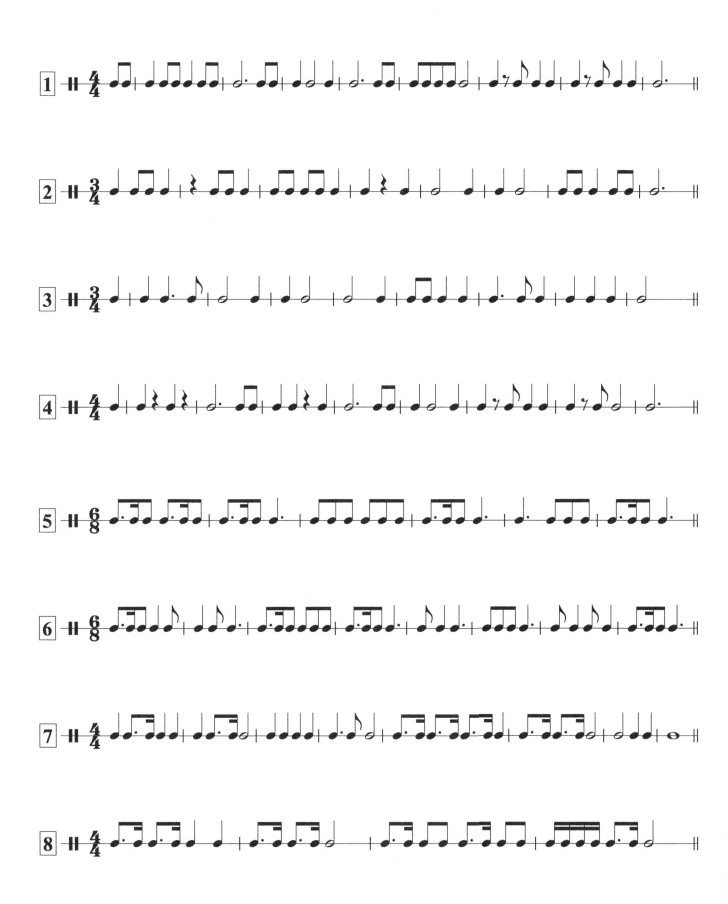

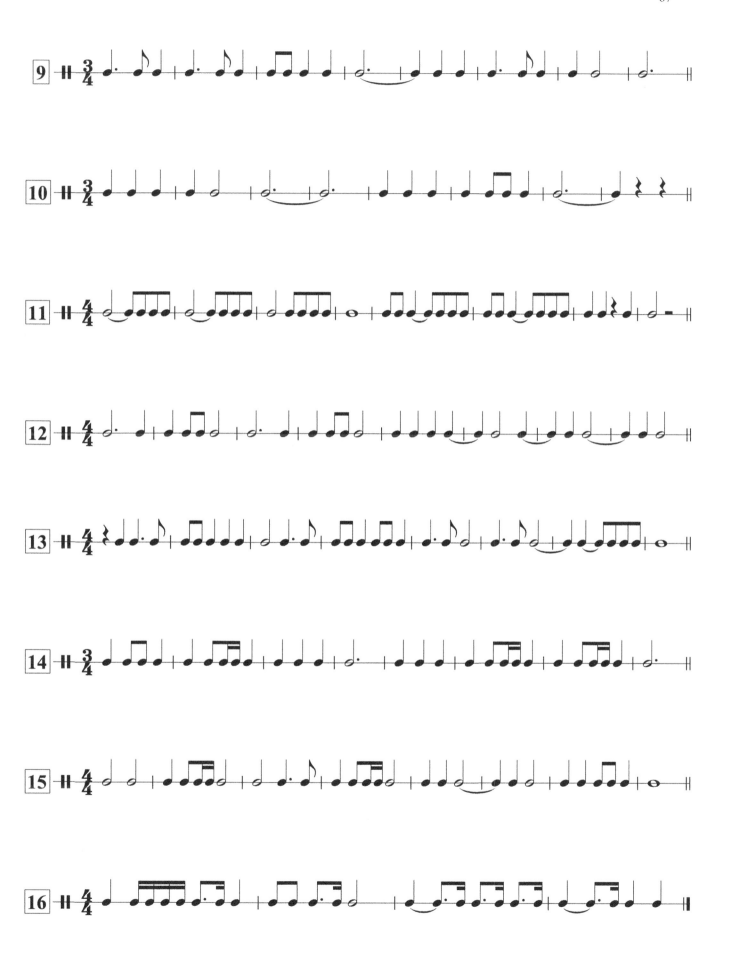

Unit 11.1
Classical Guitar Corner Academy
Play all exercises in 5th position

F Major - 5th Position

1

Each line uses a different type of rhythmic groove.
Clap the rhythms before you play and see if you can get all three lines groovin' in time.

2

There are multiple expressive directions in this exercise but they only make musical sense when we consider the entire phrase. See if you can hear the music in your head before you play and get a feel for the musical phrase.

3

El Noi de la Mare - Traditional Catalan

4

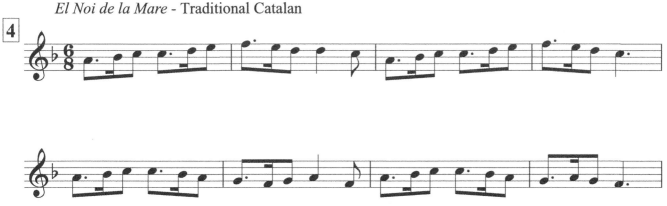

Whenever there is repetitive material, look ahead to the next measure.

5

6

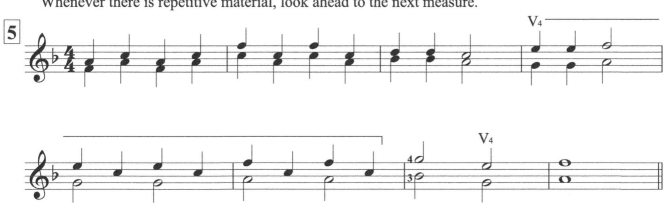

Unit 11.2
Classical Guitar Corner Academy
Play all exercises in 5th position

F Major - 5th Position

1

2

Mi Chacra - Traditional Argentine
Decide on an achieveable tempo to sight-read this melody and clap the rhythm before you play.
The "X" note-heads indicate percussion and it is up to you how to make the percussive sound.
Just make sure your hands can get back to playing position in time.

3

Scarborough Fair - Traditional English

Take a slow tempo and when in doubt, drop out!

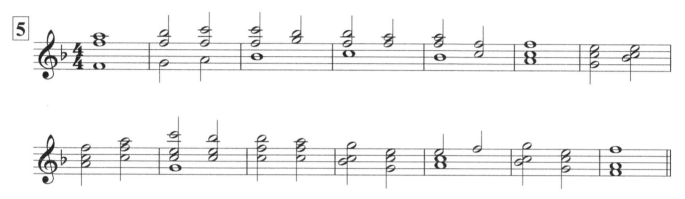

The chords in this exercise are not too common, so take a *very* slow tempo in order to look ahead.

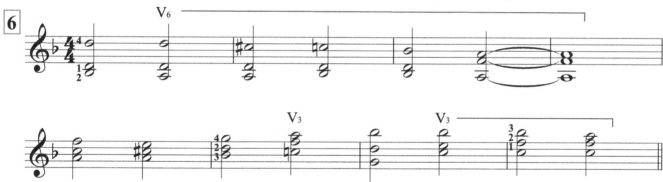

These arpeggios use the same chords as in the exercise above. Read them as two-beat chunks.

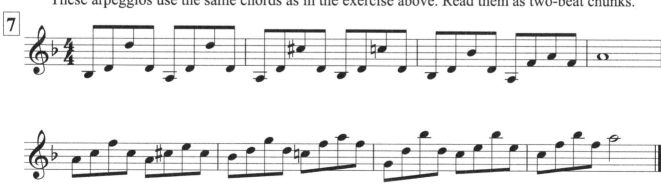

Unit 11.3
Classical Guitar Corner Academy
Play all exercises in 5th position

Bb Major - 5th Position

The horizontal line above or below a note head indicates *legato* whereas a dot indicates *staccato*.
Read through the exercise before you play and see if you can get a feel for the articulation.

This musical phrase has "sentential structure". Simply put, it is two short ideas that are very similar and one long idea that is twice as long as a short idea. Look for the dynamic and pitch similarity in the first two ideas and take note of the dynamic markings in the third part of the phrase before you play.

Skye Boat Song - Traditional Scottish

This is a challenging passage because of the key and the fingering. Sight-read to the best of your ability then take some time to create an optimal fingering for this passage.

Unit 11.4
Classical Guitar Corner Academy
Play all exercises in 5th position

G Major - 5th Position with extensions

1

Scan over this passage to get clear on the various tonal and dynamic directions.

2

My Bonnie Lies Over the Ocean - Traditional Scottish

Play these chords in free time. As soon as you have played a chord (correct notes or not) move your eyes to the next chord and only move your fingers when you have figured out the notes to play.

Unit 12.1
Classical Guitar Corner Academy
Play all exercises in 4th position

E Major - 4th position

This passage uses a very common musical device found in classical guitar music: *ostinato*. Identify the ostinato in each line and then focus on the moving part. Keep the *ostinato* very soft so that the moving part can be sounded clearly as the melody.

The Mallow Fling - Irish Traditional

4th Street Groove

Moderato

Unit 12.2

Classical Guitar Corner Academy
Play all exercises in 4th position

E Major - 4th position

1

2 *Maestoso*

3

O Mio Babbino Caro - Giacomo Puccini

How's the Serenity?

Choose a calm tempo to match the title and let notes ring out when possible.

Even though the rhythm is written with sixteenth notes you can control the sight-reading difficulty by your choice of tempo.

4

morendo

Unit 12.3
Classical Guitar Corner Academy
Play all exercises in 4th position

A Major - 4th position

There are many different musical instructions present in this passage. Take a minute to go over the music and aim to bring as much musical character into the passage from the first reading.

Danny Boy - Irish Traditional
This melody includes a leap to C# on the first string, ninth fret, in measure thirteen that briefly
takes you out of position. Figure out your fingering for this moment before you play.

Play these chords in free time and practice moving your eyes ahead to the next chord as soon as
you have played. Take a slow tempo and don't be afraid to drop notes out. You will find that
several chords can go into fifth position.

Unit 12.4
Classical Guitar Corner Academy
Play all exercises in 4th position

A Major - 4th position

Train of Thought

Reduce the challenge of this passage by taking some time to look over the score. Look at the repeated sections and map out the form of the piece. Clap through the accented rhythms. Play through the first chord shape in each measure and notice that chords do not change within a measure.

In an English Country Garden - English Traditional
Up for a challenge? After reading this melody, play it again an octave lower in the same position.

Unit 13.1
Classical Guitar Corner Academy
Play all exercises in 4th and 5th position

A Minor - 4th and 5th position

Shifting between positions as you sight-read can be challenging. In this lesson we will begin by combining the fourth and fifth positions. There are many different options that will work for each passage and your ability to look ahead in the music will help with shifting choices.

1

Vocalise the rhythm of this melody with its staccato articulations before you play.
Take note of the anacrusis and upper mordent.

2

Yablochko (Little Apple) - Russian Traditional
The articulation and rests in this melody contribute greatly to the feel of this Russian melody.
See if you can hear the rhythm and articulation in your head before you play.
This uses and extension to A# at the beginning of the third system.

March
Chordal textured in the upper positions can be challenging so use a slow tempo
to help you maintain the pulse and drop out notes if necessary.

Unit 13.2
Classical Guitar Corner Academy
Play all exercises in 4th and 5th position

A Minor - 4th and 5th position

After you have read the music in this lesson you can go back and add in fingering. This will help to develop your fingerboard knowledge and help you decide on the best ways to shift between positions.

1

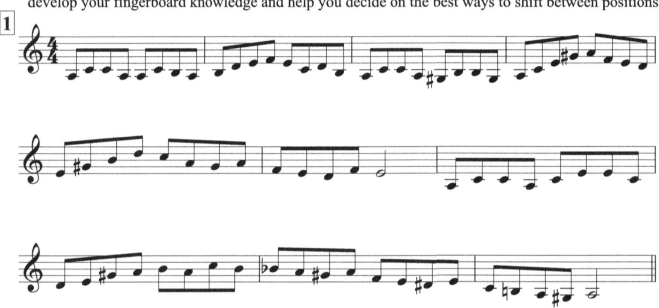

This passage features a common musical texture where a melody is sewn into arpeggios. The melody is made clear by using separate stems. Aim to bring out the melody and subdue the accompaniment.

2

rit.

Arpeggione Sonata Mvt.1 Theme - Franz Schubert

El Murciélago
Have a look through the music and see if you can identify some common harmonies that appear in the key of A minor. You will find that the dominant harmony tends to shift into fourth position. Use open strings for bass notes when appropriate.

Unit 13.3
Classical Guitar Corner Academy
Play all exercises in 4th and 5th position

D Harmonic Minor - 4th and 5th position

Sacred Chant
Scan the score to START the right way.
Make your first reading as musical as possible.

Unit 13.4
Classical Guitar Corner Academy
Play all exercises in 4th and 5th position

D Harmonic Minor - 4th and 5th position

Phantasm

Before you start scan the passage for any unusual notes so that you don't get caught off guard!
Beware, this is a difficult passage to sight-read.

Lento

El Condor Pasa - Daniel Alomía Robles
This melody contains some challenging rhythms. Take sixty seconds before you play to work on these rhythms separately. Use clapping and subdivision to help you.

3

Tanguero
Scan the score to START the right way.

4

www.classicalguitarcorner.com

Grade 6 Rhythms
Classical Guitar Corner Academy

Unit 14.1
Classical Guitar Corner Academy
Play all exercises in 2nd position

D Major - 2nd position

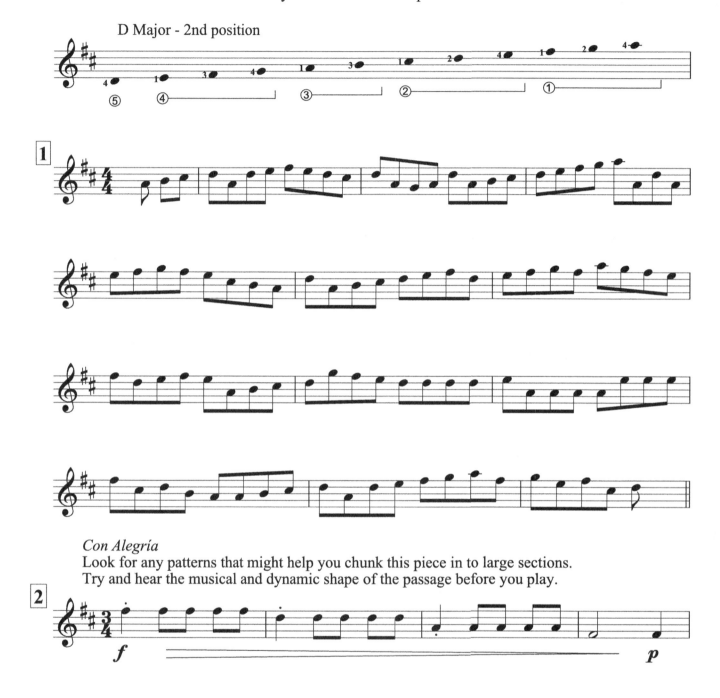

Con Alegría
Look for any patterns that might help you chunk this piece in to large sections.
Try and hear the musical and dynamic shape of the passage before you play.

Lauf der Weit - Edvard Grieg
Choose your starting tempo based on the 16th note passages in this melody. Also, note the full bar of rest and *ritardando* in the third system.

3

Moderato
Stay in second position for this melody but use open strings when it makes playing easier.

4

Largo
Stay in second position for this melody but use open strings when it can make playing easier.

5

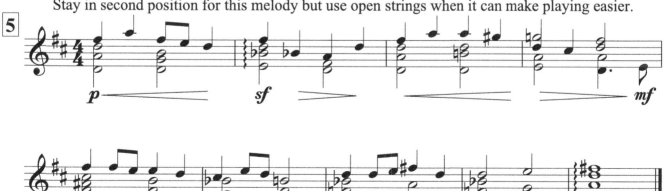

Unit 14.2
Classical Guitar Corner Academy
Play all exercises in 2nd position

D Major - 2nd position

The Hidden Cave
Use the opening trills in this passage to create a feeling of suspense and drama.
After the opening keep the legato passage as smooth and eerie as possible by playing all the slurs.

Molto legato.

Toreador, from Carmen - Georges Bizet
Shift to first position in measures 14 - 16 as indicated.

3

1st position ⎯⎯⎯⎯⎯⎯⎯

Play this passage at a brisk tempo to achieve a light and bouncy feel. However, take into account the eighth-note runs when selecting your tempo. Use open strings freely while staying in position.

4

rall.

Julia Enamorada (Barcorolle)
Use open strings in this passage to make the fingering easier and also to allow resonance.

5

rall.

Unit 14.3
Classical Guitar Corner Academy
Play all exercises in 2nd position

G Major - 2nd position

Fine

1

D.C. al Fine

The Void

Keep the pulse very slow and steady throughout to make a mysterious atmosphere.
Make sure to keep counting through the rests and use repeated notes to look ahead.

2

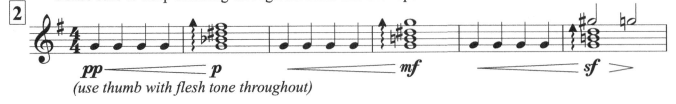

pp —————— *p* ————— *mf* ———— *sf* >

(use thumb with flesh tone throughout)

pp pizz. -

vib.

ppp

Eine Kleine Nachtmusik - Wolfgang Amadeus Mozart

3

This passage is mostly in second position but you will find yourself having to move out of position in measure five.

4

Unit 14.4
Classical Guitar Corner Academy
Play all exercises in 2nd position

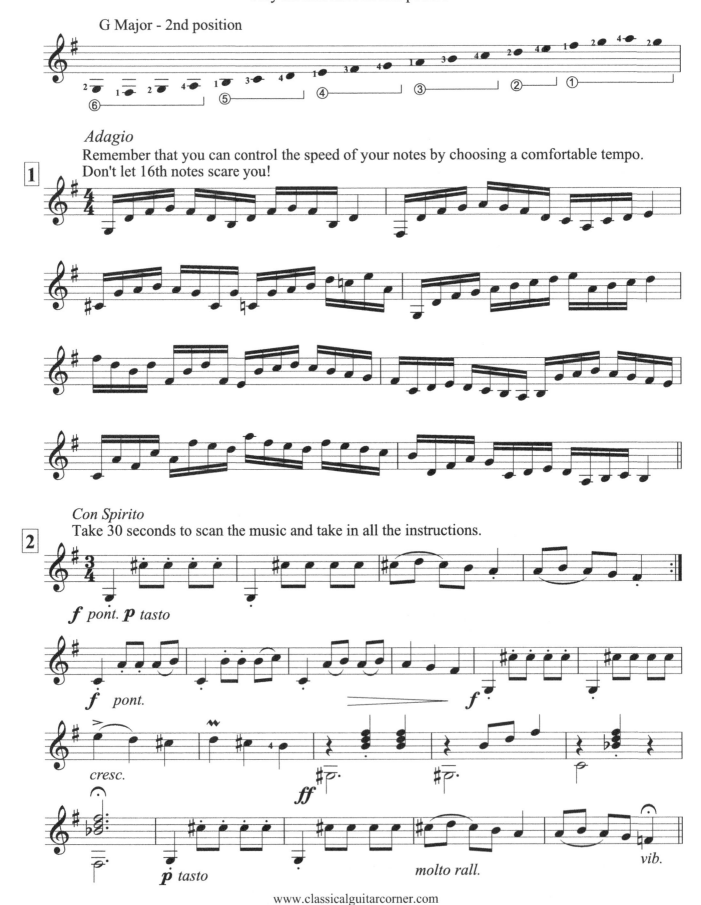

Adagio
Remember that you can control the speed of your notes by choosing a comfortable tempo.
Don't let 16th notes scare you!

Con Spirito
Take 30 seconds to scan the music and take in all the instructions.

Judas Maccabaeus - George Frideric Handel

A Fondness of Rain (In the style of Eric Satie)

umbrellas in slow motion

drop by drop

Unit 14.5
Classical Guitar Corner Academy
Play all exercises in 2nd position

B Natural Minor - 2nd position

The musical challenge in this passage is to sustain the contrapuntal voices that join the texture. Use open strings and barres to help you and note that some bass A# notes will need to be in first position. Don't forget: when in doubt, drop out!

Prelude, from L'Arlésienne Suite No. 1 - Georges Bizet

Unit 15.1
Classical Guitar Corner Academy
Play all exercises in 2nd, 4th, and 5th position
There are no scales in this unit because we explore a variety of keys in each lesson.

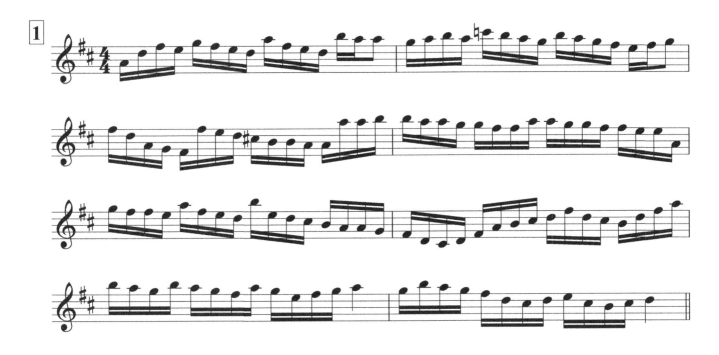

The Tired Cowboy
Swing the eighth notes in this piece to create a slow "American Western" feel.
Feel free to use open strings in the melody and bass but remain between second and fifth position.

Concerto for Lute, 2nd Mvt - Antonio Vivaldi
Second, Fourth, and Fifth Position Combined

Modal Musings
Use open strings freely but stay in 2nd and 5th position.

rall.

Unit 15.2
Classical Guitar Corner Academy
Play all exercises in 2nd, 4th, and 5th position

1

A Tricky Conversation

To sustain all the notes as indicated in the score would most likely require some thoughtful fingering. Here in the world of sight-reading we have to let go of perfection and just do the best we can.

2

Prelude - George Handel

m

3

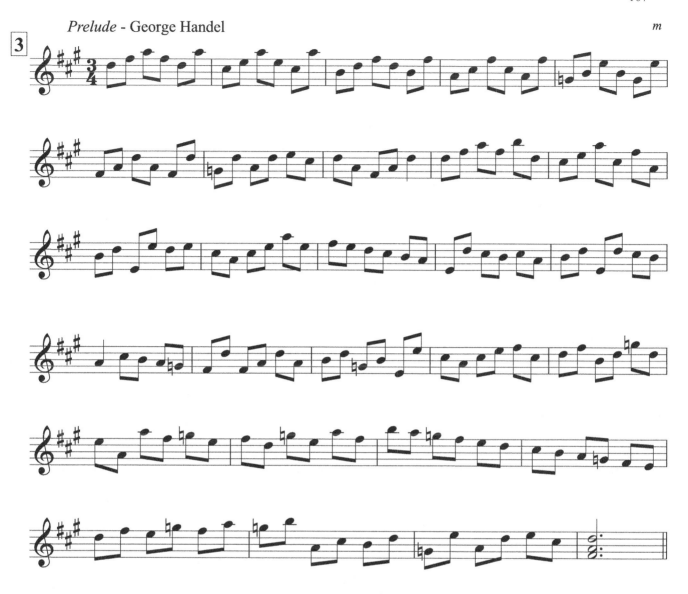

Un Petite Jazz

Many of the chords found in jazz are less familiar to classical guitarists. Use your sight-reading skills to decide what is important and what you can drop out if needed.

4

Unit 15.3
Classical Guitar Corner Academy
Play all exercises in 2nd, 4th, and 5th position

Remembering Roland

Play the bass line starting on the fouth string using the flesh of the thumb. Aim for the sound of a slow jazz ballad with double bass. You will notice dynamic markings above and below the staff. These are indicating the dynamic balance between the melody, accompaniment, and bass.

2nd Movement of Winter from the Four Seasons - Antonio Vivaldi
Although slurs are indicated in the music you may not be able to play them depending on what position you find yourself in at the time.

A State of Flow
Take a comforable tempo and keep the music as legato as possible.

Grade 7 Rhythms
Classical Guitar Corner Academy

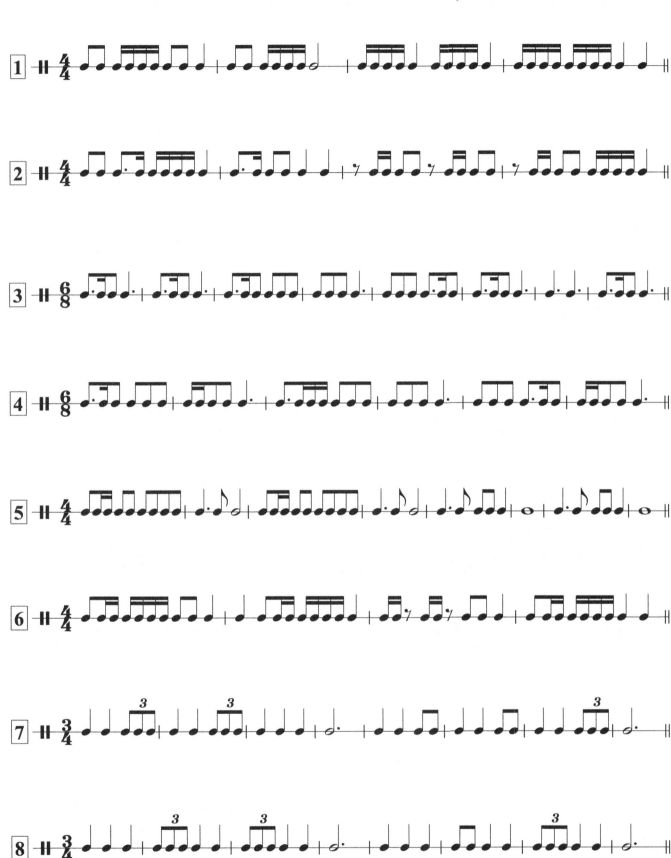

Unit 16.1
Classical Guitar Corner Academy
Play all exercises in 7th position

G Major - 7th Position

In this lesson we will dial back the difficulty as you explore higher positions.

1

Scherzo
Make this music light and playful and take a good scan of the score before you play.

2

Theme from the Unfinished Symphony - Franz Schubert
Allegro Moderato

Unit 16.2
Classical Guitar Corner Academy
Play all exercises in 7th position

D Major - 7th Position

In measure five you will see the unusual dynamic marking *f/p*. This indicates to play different dynamics on the repeated section. *Forte* the first time and *piano* on the repeat.

La Volta - Michael Praetorius

Use open strings for the bass notes where appropriate.

Unit 16.3
Classical Guitar Corner Academy
Play all exercises in 7th position

Ballet - Michael Praetorius
If you scan the score you will notice that there is actually a key change half way through this melody. Take a minute to look ahead and see which notes will change.

If this passage poses too much of a challenge simply play "divisi" and choose to play either the upper or lower voice. This can be a useful approach in ensemble music.

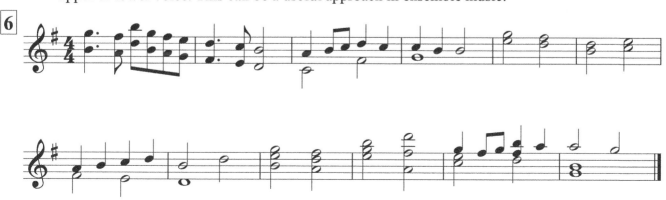

Unit 16.4

Classical Guitar Corner Academy
Play all exercises in 7th position

1

Shift up the first string into ninth position to access the notes needed in this passage.

2

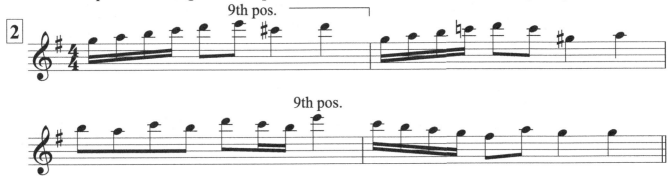

Challenge yourself to take this passage at a faster tempo.
Identify any arpeggios and scales before you begin.

3

Scan through this passage before playing to identify the three chord shapes used in the music.

4

Dodi Li - Traditional Hebrew
Up for a challenge? On each repeat play the line down an octave in seventh position.

Unit 17.1
Classical Guitar Corner Academy
Play all exercises in 9th position

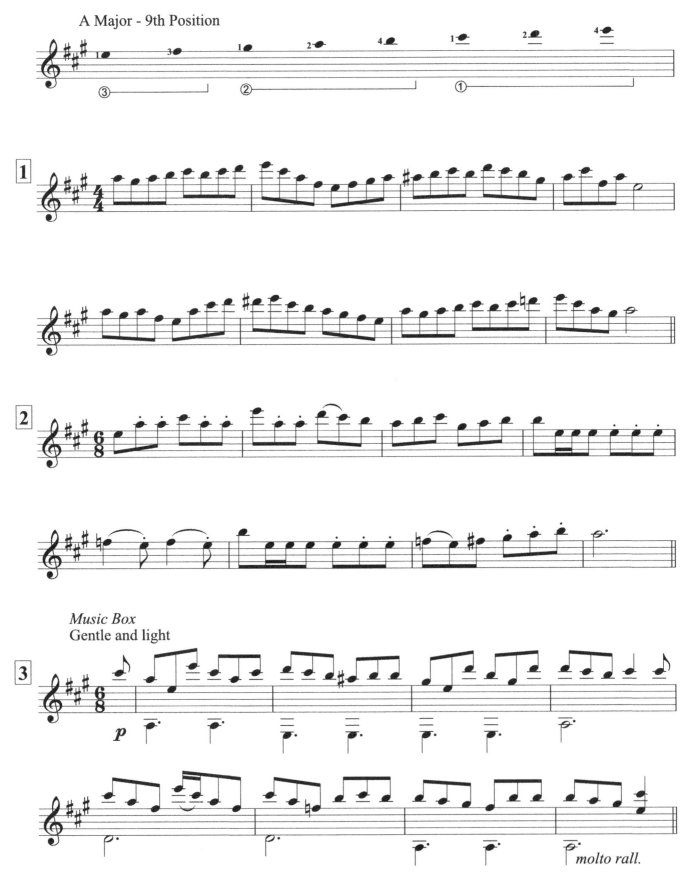

A Major - 9th Position

Music Box
Gentle and light

molto rall.

Sonata K.3 - W.A. Mozart

Unit 17.2
Classical Guitar Corner Academy
Play all exercises in 9th position

E Major - 9th Position

Choose a tempo that makes sight-reading easy. It will also help if you think of the sixteenth-note subdivisions and you count-in.

4

Wiegenlied - Johannes Brahms

5

6

7

Unit 17.3
Classical Guitar Corner Academy
Play all exercises in 9th position

Jupiter - Gustav Holst

Use open strings as needed and when in doubt, drop out.

Unit 17.4
Classical Guitar Corner Academy
Play all exercises in 9th position

The Swan - Saint Saens
This melody will require several extensions in ninth position.

4

Tremolo technique can look intimidating to read on the page but the repeated note is just one pitch. By chunking this information we can read each half-beat as a pair of notes.

5

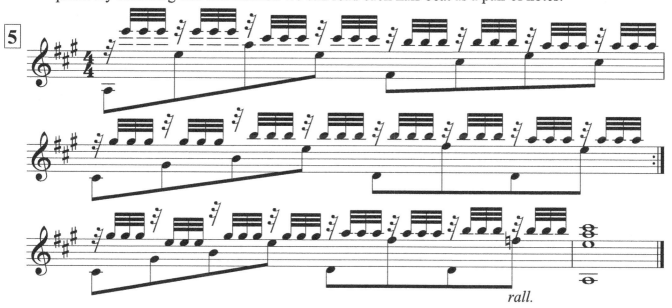

rall.

Unit 18.1
Classical Guitar Corner Academy
Mixed positions and keys

Sight-reading with all positions available to you makes shifting choices very important.
Looking ahead in the music will be the best way to shift fluently. You will develop a good sense
for when to shift between positions as you gain more experience.
All positions

Play this passage in ninth position except in measure four.
The key to unlocking this syncopated melody is to feel the groove of the piece.
Spend some time working out the rhythm before you play.
9th position

Theme from Swan Lake - Pyotr Tchaikovsky
7th position

Lesson 9 - Napoléon Coste
Use open strings to help you shift between ninth position and lower positions.
Use the fingering in the first two measures as a guide.
All positions

Unit 18.2
Classical Guitar Corner Academy
Mixed positions and keys

All positions

Minuet - Luigi Boccherini
5th position and above

Theme from Clarinet Concerto K.622 - Wolfgang Amadeus Mozart
All positions

Prelude No.11 - Francisco Tárrega
All positions. Be sure to scan the score before you start to notice an important detail!

Unit 18.3
Classical Guitar Corner Academy
Mixed positions and keys

All positions

Meditation from Thais - Jules Massenet
9th position and above

Barcarolle Op.51 No. 1 - Napoléon Coste
All positions

Grade 8 Rhythms
Classical Guitar Corner Academy

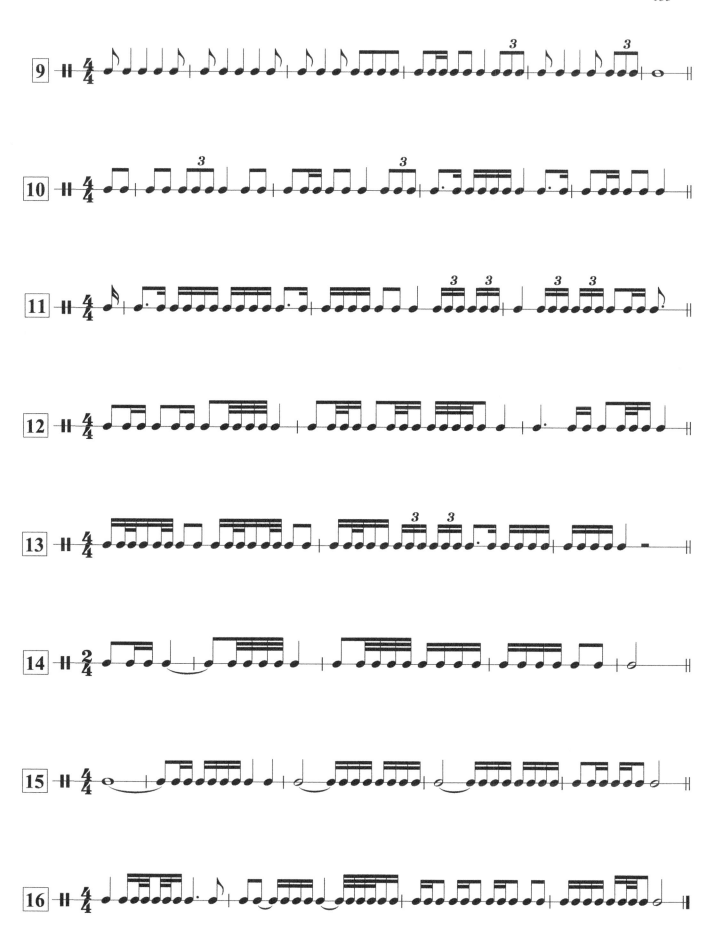

135

Unit 19.1
Classical Guitar Corner Academy
Mixed positions and keys

Theme from Violin Concerto BWV 1041 - Johann Sebastian Bach
7th and 6th positions combined

El Choclo - Angel Villoldo
2nd, 4th, 5th, and 7th positions combined

2

Unit 19.2
Classical Guitar Corner Academy
Mixed positions and keys

Bardinerie BWV 1067 - Johann Sebastian Bach
All Positions

#37 from Ghiribizzi - Niccolò Paganini
All positions

Unit 19.3
Classical Guitar Corner Academy
Mixed positions and keys

Air on a G String BWV 1068 - Johann Sebastian Bach
Keep a strong quarter note pulse in your head as you read through this slow masterpiece.
7th Position
Adagio

Lesson 24 - Napoléon Coste

Unit 20.1
Classical Guitar Corner Academy
Mixed positions and keys

Fugue BWV 1005 - Johann Sebastian Bach
All positions

1

Prelude No. 8 - Francisco Tárrega
All positions

Unit 20.2
Classical Guitar Corner Academy
Mixed positions and keys

Presto from Sonata No. 1 BWV 1001 - Johann Sebastian Bach
All positions

Andante #31 from Ghibrizzi - Niccolò Paganini
All positions

Unit 20.3
Classical Guitar Corner Academy
Mixed positions and keys

Allemande BWV 1004 - Johann Sebastian Bach
Slurs and phrase markings are included from the original violin music but you may not be
able to include them as you sight-read. It will depend on the position in which you are playing.
All positions

Fugue BWV 1003 - Johann Sebastian Bach
All positions

Unit 20.4
Classical Guitar Corner Academy

Eventide - Catharina Pratten

Throughout this book, you have encountered music with very minimal fingering. Fingering can eliminate many of the options that are available to us when sight-reading, and it can also be used as a way to avoid reading notes themselves. Of course, this does not apply to normal repertoire editions, as reading fingering along with reading notes is an integral part of the sight-reading process. In this final piece aim to incorporate the fingerings provided by the composer as you sight-read.

All Positions

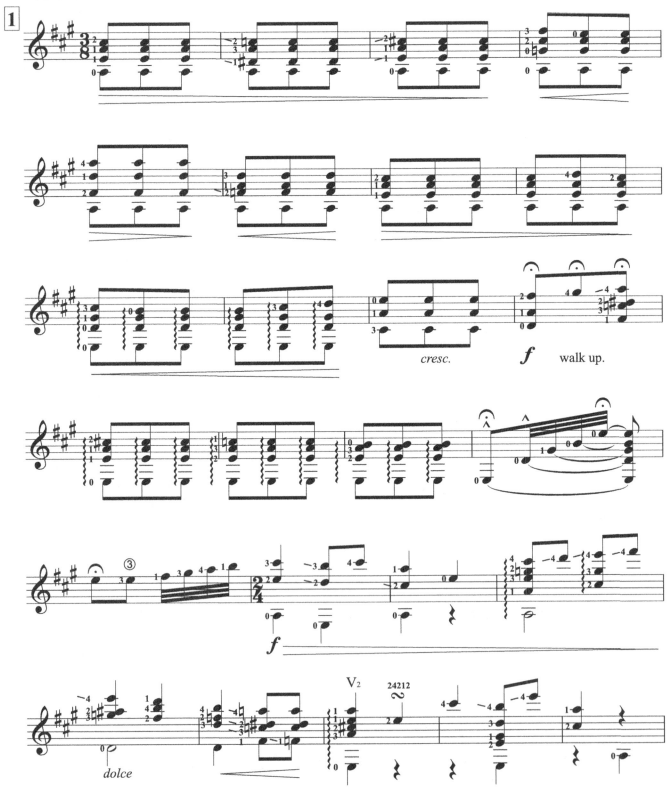

FINGERBOARD CHALLENGES

In the last section of this book you will find many of the well-known melodies that were used throughout the progressive lessons. I have transposed each melody to a new key so that you can play it in a variety of positions all over the fingerboard. It is surprising how changing a position can suddenly offer a whole new challenge!

I encourage you to play each melody in all of listed positions. Some can even be read an octave higher or lower to add yet another challenge.

Some melodies do not fit neatly into a single position. When a melody needs an extension or a brief shift out of position you will see "(ext.)" written.

Once you have exhausted this material through repetition, you can take on one last challenge: put the guitar down and write in left-hand fingerings in the position that is least familiar to you. An excellent mental challenge that works on your fingerboard knowledge.

Fingerboard Challenges
Classical Guitar Corner Academy

New World Theme - Antonin Dvořák
Second, Fifth, Seventh, Ninth

New World Theme - Antonin Dvořák
First, Second, Fourth, Seventh, Ninth

Aura Lee - Traditional American
First, Second, Fourth (ext.), Sixth, Ninth

Spring - Antonio Vivaldi
Third (ext.), Fifth, Seventh, Ninth, Eleventh

Anitra's Dance - Edvard Grieg
Because of its range and chromaticism this melody doesn't suit just one position so use the entire fingerboard when reading. Try changing your fingering each time you play.

5

Twinkle Twinkle Little Star -Traditional
First, Third, Fifth, Sixth (ext.), Eighth

6

Rujero - Gaspar Sanz
First, Second (ext.), Fourth, Fifth (ext.), Seventh, Ninth
For a challenge read this up an octave.

7

Yankee Doodle -Traditional
First, Third (ext.), Fifth, Eighth (ext.), Tenth

8

Camptown Races -Stephen Foster
First, Second, Fifth (ext.) Seventh, Ninth

9

Amazing Grace -Traditional
First, Third, Fifth, Seventh, Eighth (ext.)

10

Oh, Susanna - American Folk Song
First, Second, Fourth, Fifth (ext.), Seventh, Ninth

11

Oh, Susanna - American Folk Song
First, Second, Fourth, Fifth (ext.)

12

Simple Gifts - Joseph Brackett
Fourth, Seventh, Ninth (ext.), Eleventh

13

El Testament D'Ameila - Traditional Catalan
Fifth, Tenth (ext.)

14

Tumbalalaika- Russian Jewish Folk Song
Fifth, Seventh, Ninth (ext.)

15

Plaisir d'amour- Jean Paul Martini
Third, , Eighth (ext.), Eleventh

16

El Noi de la Mare - Traditional Catalan
Seventh, Ninth

17

Kookaburra Sits in the Old Gum Tree - Australian Traditional
First, Second, Fifth (ext.) Seventh

Mi Chacra - Argentine Traditional
First, Second (ext.), Fourth, Sixth, Seventh (ext.), Ninth Position

Scarborough Fair - Traditional English
Second, Fifth (ext.), Seventh, Ninth

Skye Boat Song - Scottish Traditional
First, Second, Fifth, Seventh, Eighth (ext.)

My Bonnie Lies Over the Ocean - Scottish Traditional
First, Second (ext.), Fourth, Sixth, Seventh (ext.), Ninth
For a challenge play this up an octave in ninth position.

The Mallow Fling - Irish Traditional
Third (ext.), Fifth, Tenth
For a challenge read this down and octave in the fifth position.

La Volta - Michael Praetorius
First, Second (ext.), Fourth, Sixth, Seventh (ext.), Ninth
For a challenge play this up an octave in ninth position.

24

Ballet - Michael Praetorius
First, Second (ext.), Fourth, Sixth and Seventh combined, Ninth

25

Dodi Li - Traditional Hebrew
Fourth (ext.), Seventh (ext.), Ninth

26

Weigenlied - Johannes Brahms
First, Fifth, Seventh

27

Jupiter - Gustav Holst
First, Second, Fourth (ext.)
For a challenge play this up an octave in seventh position.

28

The Swan - Saint Saens
First, Second (ext.), Fifth (ext.), Seventh (ext. and open strings)
For a challenge play this up an octave in seventh position.

Yablochko (Little Apple) - Russian Traditional
First, Second, Fifth (ext.), Seventh Position (slurs are not possible in some positions)

Piano Concerto No.3 Theme - Sergei Rachmaninoff
Seventh (ext.), Ninth (ext.)
For a challenge play this down an octave in first position.

O Mio Babbino Caro - Giacomo Puccini
Third (ext.), Fifth, Tenth Position

In an English Country Garden - English Traditional
First, Second (ext.), Fourth, Sixth, Ninth (ext.)

35

Eine Kleine Nachtmusik - W.A. Mozart
Fifth Position (*shift out of position briefly to play the high D in measure 11)

36

El Condor Pasa - Daniel Alomía Robles
Fourth and Fifth Position combined

37

El Condor Pasa - Daniel Alomía Robles
Fourth and Fifth Position combined
Use the open sixth string for low E as indicated

38

Danny Boy - Irish Traditional
First Position, Second Position, Fourth Position, Seventh Position (ext.)

39

Danny Boy - Irish Traditional
First Position, Fourth Position, Sixth Position, Ninth Position (ext.)

40

Prelude, from Carmen - Georges Bizet
Fourth and Fifth Position (ext.) combined

41

Fine

D.C. al Fine

Toreador, from Carmen - Georges Bizet
First, Second (ext.), Fourth and Fifth combined, Seventh (ext.)

42

Prelude, from L'Arlésienne Suite No. 1 - Georges Bizet
First, Second, Fifth Position (ext.)

43

2nd Movement of Winter from the Four Seasons - Antonio Vivaldi
Eighth and Ninth positions combined
For a challenge play this down an octave in first position.

44

Theme from Swan Lake - Pyotr Tchaikovsky
First, Second (ext.), Fourth (ext.), Sixth (ext.), Ninth (ext.)

45

Concerto for Lute, 2nd Mvt - Antonio Vivaldi
First, Second, and Fourth Position

46

Minuet - Luigi Boccherini
First, Second (ext.), Fourth and Fifth combined

47

Theme from Clarinet Concerto K.622 - Wolfgang Amadeus Mozart
First through Fifth Position combined

48

Meditation from Thais - Jules Massenet
First*, Second*, Fourth*, Seventh*
*This soaring melody has a large range so you can center yourself around each position but eventually you will have to shift out of position. This melody requires a drop D tuning.

49

Theme from Violin Concerto BWV 1041 - Johann Sebastian Bach
First, Fifth (with several shifts out of position to reach the bass range)

50

Bardinerie BWV 1067 - Johann Sebastian Bach
First, Second (with open strings and extensions)

Presto from Sonata No. 1 BWV 1001 - Johann Sebastian Bach
All Positions

52

El Choclo - Angel Villoldo
All positions

53

More Sight-Reading Challenges
www.classicalguitarcorner.com/sight-reading

The never ending search for more material

Sight-reading has an inherent challenge in that you always need fresh material to work with. At some point the material in this book will become familiar enough that it loses its usefulness. There are endless resources online where you can find new material to read but the challenge there is that it's difficult to find music that is at the appropriate level for you.

In an effort to provide ongoing resources for you to continue sight-reading I have set up a special email list where I will send out new materials as I come across them. If there is sufficient interest I will also consider writing more books with sight-reading resources.

If you would like to get further resources you can sign-up here:
www.classicalguitarcorner.com/sight-reading

CGC Academy

If you enjoy learning with structured and progressive material then you will love what Classical Guitar Corner Academy has to offer. Sight-reading is just one part of our curriculum that also features solo repertoire, duets, practice routines, scale and arpeggios, theory, technique, and musicianship.

In addition to the curriculum you will discover a supportive and welcoming community of guitarists that share your passion for music.

Find out more at : www.classicalguitarcorner.com/join-cgc

Made in the USA
Las Vegas, NV
25 February 2024

86263643R00096